The New Classic **Cook**

Fast & Fabulous

Delicious Meals Without the Wait

Time Inc. Home Entertainment

Contents

Time-saving Tips

Think Ahead
Planning is the key to saving time in the kitchen. Decide what you're going to eat for the coming week, buy all your dry and canned ingredients (fresh meat, fish, fruit and vegetables can be bought as you need them) and do as much preparation as you can in advance.

Sauces can be cooked and refrigerated or frozen, and meat and fish can be marinated overnight ready to quickly stir-fry the next night. A well-planned weekly menu will save you hours every week.

Plan B
Not everyone is this well-organized, so here are some suggestions for the more haphazard cook.

• Keep your pantry well-stocked with staples. If you have the makings of a simple pasta dish or a vegetable curry always on hand, you can keep your family well-fed and happy.

• Make sure you have supplies of fast-cooking rice, noodles, polenta and couscous and so you can knock out a side dish in no time at all.

• Get to know stir-fries (and invest in a wok). You can make a delicious and nutritious stir-fry for four in under 15 minutes. And the more you use this method of cooking, the more you'll experiment with different flavors, expanding your repertoire and increasing your enjoyment.

• Buy tender, choice cuts of meat. These may seem extravagant at first, but if time is short, you'll see what a saving it is to buy quick-cooking meat. You'll spend less time trimming fat and gristle from it too.

• Eat more fish. Fish fillets cook very quickly and are a healthy low-fat food. Fish doesn't have to be fried or grilled.

Try a fish stew, cooked in a tomato and vegetable sau and served with bread. (The sauce can be made in advan and all you have to do is heat it up, add chopped fish, co for a few minutes and serve sprinkled with parsley.)

• Keep dried herbs in the pantry to use when you can't g fresh. One teaspoon of dried herbs is equivalent to o tablespoon fresh.

• Use packaged products judiciously. Bottled tomato pas sauce, minced garlic and curry pastes are all time-savers a many are of very good quality. Read labels carefully befc you buy to make sure you're not buying a jar of preservative

The Microwave
Use your microwave oven to defrost frozen food, to rehe casseroles and other cooked food, and to cook vegetabl and fish.

Meals for one or two can be very quickly cooked in t microwave—a baked potato takes four to six minute instead of the usual hour in the oven. But cooking rice pasta for four people in the microwave takes about t same time as it does in a saucepan on the stove.

Freezing food
One of the best ways to save time in the kitchen is to co twice as much as you need for one dish and freeze the re You can't freeze everything of course, but most casserol pies, sauces and soups freeze very well and taste just good (some taste even better) when reheated.

• Label and date everything you freeze.

• Freeze lemon and lime juice in ice-cube containers th re-package in freezer bags. Do the same with stock, a drop one or two cubes as required into sauces, soups a vegetable dishes for extra flavor.

Store shrimp shells and other offensive-smelling trash such as meat scraps in the freezer until garbage day.

Chop and fry about eight onions and eight cloves of garlic in olive oil; divide among four small plastic bags. They don't freeze solid so you can just drop the contents into a frying pan and take it from there.

Freeze fresh herbs, chilies and ginger either dry in freezer bags or finely chopped in ice-cube trays, barely covered with water. Wash and dry the herbs well first; peel the ginger but freeze in pieces—it grates more easily when frozen. Transfer the frozen cubes to freezer bags for storage.

◆ Milk, bread, butter and cream can all be frozen. Cut butter into portions before freezing.

◆ Leftover cooked rice and cooked dried (not fresh) pasta freeze very well.

Pantry Basics: A supply of staples—canned, bottled and frozen foods—will mean that even if you didn't have time to shop at lunchtime you'll still be able to produce a tasty meal for dinner.

artichoke hearts, bottled	kidney beans, canned	REFRIGERATOR
breadcrumbs	lentils, red	butter, margarine
broth, canned, chicken and beef	mustard	cheese
butter beans, canned	noodles	cream
cajun seasoning	nutmeg, ground	eggs
cannellini beans, canned	oil (olive, vegetable)	milk
chili powder	olives, black	sour cream
chili sauce	oyster sauce	yogurt
cinnamon sticks	pasta rice (long-grain, arborio)	
corn kernels, canned	salmon, canned	FREEZER
creamed corn, canned	sesame seeds	bacon
coconut cream and milk	soy sauce	bread
coriander, ground	sugar (white, brown)	breadcrumbs, stale
corn chips	sun-dried tomatoes	pine nuts
cornstarch	paprika, sweet	pizza crusts
couscous	Tabasco sauce	
cumin, ground	tomatoes, canned	FRUIT & VEGETABLES
curry powder	tomato paste	carrots
flour	tomato pasta sauce	chiles
garbanzos, canned	tuna, canned	garlic
ginger	turmeric, ground	ginger
ground herbs, dried	vinegar (balsamic, wine)	lemons, limes
honey	wine	potatoes

Chicken

Chicken with Thyme Butter Sauce

preparation time 5 minutes

cooking time 20 minutes

4 boneless, skinless chicken breasts (1$\frac{1}{2}$ lbs.)
flour
$\frac{1}{4}$ cup olive oil
1 stick butter
1$\frac{1}{2}$ tbsp. chopped fresh thyme
2 scallions, chopped
$\frac{1}{4}$ cup lemon juice

Toss chicken in flour, shake away excess. Heat oil and half the butter in large skillet, add chicken to skillet; cook over medium heat 10 minutes or until tender. Drain on paper towels; keep warm. Discard pan juices.

Heat remaining butter in same skillet; cook thyme and scallions, stirring, over medium heat, two minutes or until scallions are soft. Stir in lemon juice, cook three minutes.

Drizzle chicken with sauce; serve with zucchini, if desired.

SERVES 4

per serving: 48.7g fat; 594 calories
tip: This recipe is best made close to serving time.

Chicken with Almond Sauce

preparation time 15 minutes
cooking time 25 minutes

1/4 cup olive oil
1/2 cup orange juice
3 cloves garlic, crushed
6 boneless, skinless chicken breasts (2 lbs.)
3 small fennel bulbs (about 2 lbs.)
2 medium red onions
1 1/2 tbsp. olive oil, extra

ALMOND SAUCE
1 1/2 tbsp. olive oil
1/4 cup stale breadcrumbs
3/4 cup finely ground almonds
pinch ground cloves
1 cup chicken stock
3 tbsp. dry white wine
1/4 cup heavy cream

Combine oil, orange juice and garlic in a medium bowl; add chicken, toss to coat in marinade. Cook chicken on a heated oiled grill pan until browned on both sides and cooked through.

Meanwhile, cut fennel and onions into wedges. Heat extra oil in large skillet; cook fennel and onion, stirring, until onions are soft and lightly browned. Remove from heat, cover to keep warm.

Serve chicken with fennel mixture and almond sauce.

Almond Sauce: Heat oil in medium skillet, add breadcrumbs; cook, stirring, until lightly browned. Add almonds and cloves; cook, stirring, until lightly browned. Gradually add combined stock and wine, stir over medium heat until mixture is smooth; bring to a boil. Remove from heat, stir in cream.

SERVES 6

per serving: 36.8g fat; 548 calories
tip: This recipe is best made close to serving time.

Saucy Chicken in Yogurt

preparation time 10 minutes
(plus standing time)

cooking time 20 minutes

1^3/4 lbs. chicken tenderloins
16 oz. bottled satay sauce
2 large onions
1^1/2 tbsp. olive oil
8 oz. cherry tomatoes, halved
^{1}/3 cup shredded fresh basil
1 cup plain yogurt
3 tbsp. sweet Thai chili sauce

Combine chicken and ^{1}/2 cup of the satay sauce in large bowl; let stand five minutes.

Heat oil in large skillet; cook chicken, in batches, until cooked through. Cover to keep warm.

Meanwhile, cut onions into wedges. Heat oil in same skillet; cook onions, stirring, until soft. Add remaining satay sauce, tomatoes and basil; cook, stirring, about five minutes or until heated through.

Return chicken to skillet; stir to coat with satay sauce mixture.

Combine yogurt and chili sauce; serve chicken with sauce.

SERVES **4**

per serving: 48.3g fat; 827 calories
tips: Chicken can be marinated several hours or overnight; cover, refrigerate. Cook close to serving time.

Lemon Chicken Phyllo Pockets

preparation time 15 minutes
(plus cooling time)

cooking time 30 minutes

2 tbsp. butter
1$^1/_2$ tbsp. vegetable oil
4 boneless, skinless chicken breasts (1$^1/_2$ lbs.)
8 sheets phyllo pastry
5 tbsp. butter, melted, extra
1$^1/_2$ tbsp. whole-grain mustard
1$^1/_2$ tbsp. chopped fresh cilantro

LEMON SAUCE
1$^1/_2$ tbsp. lemon juice
1$^1/_2$ tbsp. chopped fresh cilantro
1$^1/_2$ tbsp. grated fresh ginger
$^1/_2$ cup heavy cream

Preheat oven to 350°F. Grease baking sheet. Heat butter and oil in medium skillet; cook chicken, turning occasionally, until lightly browned. Remove from skillet; drain and cool. Reserve skillet, with juices, for sauce.

To prevent phyllo from drying out, cover sheets with parchment paper and a damp dish towel until ready to use. Place one sheet of phyllo on cutting board, brush with some of the extra butter. Top with another layer of phyllo, brush with butter. Fold phyllo in half; place a chicken breast in center of one end of phyllo. Spread chicken with some of the mustard and sprinkle with a little cilantro. Fold sides of phyllo over chicken, roll up to form a pocket. Repeat with remaining phyllo, butter, chicken, mustard and cilantro.

Place pockets on prepared baking sheet; brush with remaining extra butter. Bake, uncovered, 20 minutes or until golden. Serve pockets with lemon sauce and, if desired, boiled new potatoes and asparagus.

Lemon Sauce: add ingredients to reserved juices in skillet. Stir constantly over medium heat until reduced by half.

SERVES 4

per serving: 44.9g fat; 652 calories
tip: Chicken pockets can be prepared
several hours ahead; cover, refrigerate.

Chicken Burgers

preparation time 10 minutes

cooking time 15 minutes

1 lb. ground chicken
1 medium zucchini, grated coarsely
3 medium carrots, grated coarsely
3 tbsp. flour
2 tsp. Cajun seasoning
4 whole-wheat hamburger buns
2 medium tomatoes, seeded, chopped finely
$1\frac{1}{2}$ tbsp. finely chopped fresh chives
2 tsp. olive oil
4 large lettuce leaves
$\frac{1}{3}$ cup sour cream
$\frac{1}{4}$ tsp. hot paprika

Combine chicken, zucchini, carrot, flour and seasoning in large bowl; shape mixture by hand into four patties. Cook patties in large heated oiled skillet until browned on both sides and cooked through.

Meanwhile, split buns in half; toast cut sides until browned lightly. Combine tomatoes, chives and oil in small bowl.

To serve, sandwich burgers, lettuce, tomato mixture and combined sour cream and paprika between bun halves.

SERVES 4

per serving: 22.2g fat; 457 calories
tip: Uncooked patties can be stored, covered, in the refrigerator overnight or in the freezer for up to two months.

Barbecue-flavored Chicken and Onions

preparation time 10 minutes

cooking time 20 minutes

3 tbsp. lemon juice
3 tbsp. brown sugar
$1^1/_2$ tbsp. honey
1 clove garlic, crushed
$^1/_4$ cup soy sauce
2 medium onions
one $3^1/_2$ lb. rotisserie chicken, quartered

Preheat oven to 400°F.

Combine lemon juice, sugar, honey, garlic and soy sauce in small measuring cup. Cut onions into wedges. Place chicken and onion in shallow baking dish; drizzle with half the glaze mixture.

Bake, uncovered, about 20 minutes or until chicken is crisp and heated through, brushing frequently with remaining glaze mixture.

SERVES 4

per serving: 14.3g fat; 309 calories
tip: This recipe can be made a day ahead; cover, refrigerate.

Sesame Chicken with Bok Choy

preparation time 10 minutes
(plus standing time)

cooking time 10 minutes

1 1/2 lbs. boneless, skinless chicken breasts, sliced thinly
2 cloves garlic, crushed
1 1/2 tbsp. grated lemon peel
1 cup flour, approximately
2 eggs, beaten lightly
1 cup white sesame seeds
1/3 cup peanut oil
8 oz. bok choy, chopped

Combine chicken with garlic and lemon peel in large bowl; cover, refrigerate 10 minutes.

Dredge chicken in flour, shake away excess; dip chicken in egg, then press on seeds. Place chicken on baking sheet; cover, refrigerate 20 minutes.

Heat oil in large skillet; cook chicken, in batches, until browned and cooked through. Drain on paper towels.

Return chicken to skillet with bok choy; cook, tossing, until bok choy just wilts. Serve with lemon wedges, if desired.

SERVES 4

per serving: 52g fat; 795 calories
tips: Chicken can be marinated several hours or overnight; cover, refrigerate. Recipe is best cooked just before serving time.

Glazed Thai Chicken

preparation time 10 minutes

cooking time 15 minutes

8 boneless, skinless chicken thighs (2^1/$_2$ lbs.)

THAI GLAZE
^{1}/$_2$ cup sweet Thai chili sauce
1^1/$_2$ tbsp. fish sauce
1^1/$_2$ tbsp. peanut oil
1^1/$_2$ tbsp. chopped fresh cilantro
3 tbsp. lime juice
2 tsp. soy sauce

Poach chicken in large pot of simmering water for eight minutes or until almost cooked through; drain.

Cook chicken on oiled grill pan until browned on both sides and cooked through.

Meanwhile, combine ingredients for Thai glaze in small bowl, pour over chicken; cook about one minute or until chicken is glazed.

SERVES 4

per serving: 35.5g fat; 491 calories
tips: Chicken can be poached several hours ahead; cover, refrigerate. Poached chicken can also be frozen for up to two months.

Chicken and Corn with Asian Egg Sauce

preparation time 10 minutes

cooking time 20 minutes

2 eggs
1 1/2 tbsp. peanut oil
4 oz. canned creamed corn
1 1/2 tbsp. chopped fresh ginger
1 clove garlic, crushed
1 serrano chile, chopped
1 small white onion, chopped
1/2 cup chicken stock
1 1/2 lbs. boneless, skinless chicken thighs
3 1/2 oz. fresh baby corn
1 medium red bell pepper, sliced
6 scallions, sliced

Whisk eggs and one teaspoon of the oil in small measuring cup. Brush large heated skillet with a little of the remaining oil; add half of the egg mixture, swirling skillet to form a thin omelet. Remove omelet from skillet; repeat with remaining egg mixture. Roll omelets tightly; cut into thin slices.

Blend or process creamed corn, ginger, garlic, chile, white onion and stock until almost smooth.

Cut each chicken thigh into thirds. Heat remaining oil in same skillet; cook chicken, in batches, until browned and cooked through. Add baby corn and bell pepper to same skillet; cook until just tender.

Return chicken to skillet with creamed corn mixture; cook until sauce boils. Add scallions and egg roll slices; cook, tossing to combine ingredients.

SERVES 4

per serving: 20.6g fat; 395 calories
tip: This recipe best made close to serving time.

Pesto-grilled Chicken Drumsticks

preparation time 10 minutes

cooking time 15 minutes

12 chicken drumsticks (4 lbs.)
1¹/₂ tbsp. olive oil
3 tbsp. lemon juice
3 cloves garlic, crushed
1 stick butter, softened
3 tbsp. bottled pesto

We used a sun-dried tomato pesto in this recipe but you might prefer to experiment with one of the other different pesto flavors.

Make deep diagonal cuts across each chicken drumstick. Combine oil, lemon juice and garlic in large bowl; add chicken, toss to coat in marinade.

Combine butter and pesto in small bowl; press ²/₃ of the pesto mixture into cuts and all over chicken.

Cook chicken under heated broiler, brushing, occasionally, with remaining pesto mixture until browned all over and cooked through. Brush chicken with pan juices and serve.

SERVES 4

per serving: 43.8g fat; 529 calories
tip: Chicken can be cooked a day ahead; cover, refrigerate. Serve hot or cold.

Chicken and Pasta Salad

preparation time 20 minutes
(plus cooling time)

cooking time 10 minutes

2 boneless, skinless chicken breasts
8 oz. fettuccine pasta
$3^1/2$ oz. snow peas
4 oz. broccoli
2 tsp. sesame seeds, toasted
1 medium green bell pepper, sliced
6 scallions, chopped

DRESSING
$1/4$ cup lemon juice
$1^1/2$ tbsp. yellow mustard
$1^1/2$ tbsp. chopped fresh parsley
2 tsp. grated fresh ginger
$1/4$ cup water

Poach, steam or microwave chicken until tender; drain, cool, slice finely.

Cook pasta in large pot of boiling salted water, uncovered, until just tender; drain. Rinse under cold water; drain.

Drop snow peas and broccoli into small pot of boiling water, return to boil, drain; place into bowl of ice water, drain.

Whisk together ingredients for dressing. Place pasta on serving plate; top with snow peas, broccoli, bell pepper, scallions and chicken; sprinkle with sesame seeds. Add dressing just before serving.

SERVES 4

per serving: 6.6g fat; 342 calories
tips: Chicken, snow peas and broccoli can be prepared several hours ahead; cover, refrigerate. Dressing can be made several days ahead; cover, refrigerate. Assemble salad just before serving.

Light and Spicy Breaded Chicken

preparation time 10 minutes
(plus standing time)

cooking time 15 minutes

12 chicken tenderloins (2 lbs.)
1/3 cup flour
2 egg whites, beaten lightly
1/3 cup packaged breadcrumbs
1/3 cup crushed corn flakes
2 tsp. garlic salt
1 tsp. lemon pepper

Preheat oven to 425°F.

Toss chicken in flour; shake away excess. Dip chicken in egg whites, then in combined breadcrumbs, corn flakes, salt and pepper. Cover; refrigerate 15 minutes.

Place chicken in single layer on baking sheet; bake, uncovered, 15 minutes or until cooked through.

SERVES 4

per serving: 12.9g fat; 411 calories
tips: Chicken can be prepared several hours ahead; cover, refrigerate. Breaded chicken can be frozen for up to two months. Cook just before serving time.

Mango Chicken with Spinach and Sweet Potatoes

preparation time 10 minutes

cooking time 20 minutes

$1/4$ cup peanut oil
1 lb. sweet potatoes, sliced
$1^{3}/_{4}$ lbs. chicken
1 medium white onion, chopped
1 clove garlic, crushed
$1^{1}/_{2}$ tbsp. ground cumin
$1/3$ cup mango chutney
3 tbsp. lime juice
5 oz. snow peas, halved
8 oz. spinach, trimmed, chopped

Heat half the oil in large skillet; cook sweet potatoes, in batches, until just tender.

Heat remaining oil in skillet; cook chicken with onion, garlic and cumin, in batches, until chicken is browned and cooked through.

Return chicken mixture and potatoes to skillet with remaining ingredients; cook, tossing, until spinach is just wilted.

SERVES **4**

per serving: 29.6g fat; 562 calories
tip: This recipe is best made close to serving time.

Chicken Breasts in Spinach and Feta Sauce

preparation time 10 minutes

cooking time 25 minutes

3 tbsp. olive oil
4 boneless, skinless chicken breasts (1$\frac{1}{2}$ lbs.)
1 medium onion, chopped finely
2 cloves garlic, crushed
$\frac{1}{4}$ cup dry white wine
1$\frac{1}{2}$ cups heavy cream
4 oz. feta cheese, crumbled
8 oz. spinach, chopped roughly

Heat oil in large skillet; cook chicken, uncovered, until browned on both sides and cooked through. Remove from skillet; cover to keep warm.

Add onion and garlic to same skillet; cook, stirring, until onion is soft. Stir in wine. Bring to a boil; simmer, uncovered, until liquid is almost evaporated.

Add cream and cheese; simmer, uncovered, about five minutes or until sauce thickens slightly. Add spinach; stir until spinach just wilts. Top chicken with sauce.

SERVES 4

per serving: 58.7g fat; 735 calories
tip: This recipe is best made close to serving time.

Beef

Garlic Mustard Steak Salad

preparation time 15 minutes

cooking time 10 minutes

2 cloves garlic, crushed
2 lbs. top round or sirloin steak
3 tbsp. oil
3 medium carrots
1 small green cucumber, seeded
1 medium red onion, sliced

DRESSING
$1/2$ cup olive oil
$1/4$ cup white vinegar
$1^{1}/2$ tbsp. chopped fresh parsley
$1^{1}/2$ tbsp. whole-grain mustard
1 tsp. sugar

Rub garlic over both sides of steak. Heat oil in medium skillet; add steak, cook until browned on both sides and cooked as desired. Remove steak from skillet. Cut steak into strips, reserve any juices.

Meanwhile, cut carrots and cucumber into strips. Place onion in a heatproof bowl, cover with boiling water; let stand five minutes, drain.

Whisk together ingredients for dressing.

Combine steak, reserved juices, carrots, cucumber, onion and dressing in large bowl.

SERVES 4

per serving: 50.7g fat; 700 calories
tip: Salad can be made several hours ahead; cover, refrigerate.

Beef Stroganoff

preparation time 10 minutes

cooking time 20 minutes

1½ lbs. top round or sirloin steak, sliced thinly
3 tbsp. flour
1 tsp. sweet paprika
5 tbsp. butter
2 small onions, chopped finely
2 cloves garlic, crushed
8 oz. button mushrooms
1½ tbsp. lemon juice
3 tbsp. dry red wine
3 tbsp. tomato paste
1½ cups sour cream
3 tbsp. chopped fresh chives

Coat steak in combined flour and paprika; shake off excess.

Melt butter in medium skillet; cook onions and garlic, stirring constantly, over medium heat three minutes or until onions are soft. Increase heat to high; add steak gradually to skillet, stirring constantly until all steak is browned all over.

Add mushrooms, lemon juice and wine to skillet; stir until ingredients are combined. Reduce heat; cover, simmer over low heat for five minutes or until steak is tender.

Stir in tomato paste and sour cream; stir constantly over medium heat until mixture is heated through. Sprinkle with chives just before serving; serve with boiled pasta or rice, if desired.

SERVES 2

per serving: 116.9g fat; 1,525 calories
tips: Stroganoff can be made a day ahead without adding the tomato paste and sour cream; cover, refrigerate. Stroganoff can be frozen for up to two months without the mushrooms, tomato paste and sour cream; add these after reheating steak mixture.

Herbed Croquettes with Mushroom Sauce

preparation time 10 minutes

cooking time 30 minutes

1 3/4 lbs. ground beef
1 medium onion, chopped finely
3 medium carrots, grated coarsely
1 medium red bell pepper, chopped finely
2 tsp. fresh thyme
2 cloves garlic, crushed
2 eggs, beaten lightly
1/2 cup flour

2 tbsp. butter
1 1/2 tbsp. vegetable oil

MUSHROOM SAUCE
1/3 cup flour
1/3 cup dry red wine
2 cups beef stock
6 scallions, chopped finely
4 oz. button mushrooms, sliced

Combine beef, onion, carrots, bell pepper, thyme, garlic and eggs in medium bowl; mix with wooden spoon until well combined. Divide mixture into eight equal portions; roll into balls, flatten slightly into croquette shapes. Place flour in shallow bowl or plate; toss croquettes in flour, shake off excess.

Heat butter and oil in medium skillet over medium heat; cook croquettes, about 10 minutes on each side, turning several times during cooking. Drain on paper towels. Reserve pan drippings for mushroom sauce.

Make mushroom sauce. Place croquettes on serving plates, drizzle with mushroom sauce. Serve with your favorite steamed vegetables.

Mushroom Sauce: Place about five tablespoons of reserved pan drippings in small pot; add flour, stirring constantly, over medium heat one minute or until mixture browns lightly. Gradually stir in combined wine and stock; stir constantly over high heat until sauce boils and thickens. Add scallions and mushrooms; simmer two minutes.

SERVES 8

per serving: 17.2g fat; 1,323 calories
tips: Croquettes can be made a day ahead; cover, refrigerate. Uncooked and unfloured croquettes can be frozen for up to two months.

Stir-fried Mexican Beef

preparation time 20 minutes

cooking time 15 minutes

1$\frac{3}{4}$ lbs. beef tenderloin, sliced thinly
1 packet taco seasoning
1$\frac{1}{2}$ tbsp. peanut oil
1 large red onion, sliced thinly
1 medium red bell pepper, sliced thinly
1 medium yellow bell pepper, sliced thinly
4 small tomatoes (1 lb.), seeded, sliced
3 tbsp. fresh cilantro

You can use filet mignon, top round or London broil in this recipe if you prefer.

Combine beef and seasoning in medium bowl. Heat half the oil in large skillet; cook beef mixture and onion, in batches, until well browned.

Heat remaining oil in same skillet; cook bell peppers until just tender.

Return beef mixture to skillet with tomatoes and cilantro; cook until hot.

SERVES 4

per serving: 14.3g fat; 362 calories
tip: Beef can be marinated several hours ahead or overnight; cover, refrigerate.

Chili Beef and Spinach

preparation time 15 minutes

cooking time 15 minutes

2 serrano chiles, chopped
1 clove garlic, crushed
14 oz. top-round or sirloin steak, sliced thinly
$1\frac{1}{2}$ tbsp. peanut oil
1 lb. spinach, trimmed, chopped
2 tsp. teriyaki sauce
1 tsp. sugar
1 tsp. cornstarch
$\frac{1}{4}$ cup beef stock

Combine chile and garlic in large bowl; toss steak to coat in marinade.

Heat oil in large skillet; cook steak mixture, in batches, until browned all over and cooked as desired.

Add spinach to same skillet with teriyaki sauce and sugar; cook until just wilted. Add blended cornstarch and stock to skillet; stir until sauce boils and thickens.

SERVES 4

per serving: 9.9g fat; 193 calories
tip: Beef can be marinated several hours ahead or overnight; cover, refrigerate.

Gourmet Beef Burgers

preparation time 10 minutes

cooking time 15 minutes

1³/₄ lbs. ground beef
1 cup stale breadcrumbs
3 tbsp. chopped fresh flat-leaf parsley
3 tbsp. sun-dried tomato paste
1¹/₂ tbsp. olive oil
4 oz. mozzarella cheese, sliced thinly
¹/₂ cup mayonnaise
4 good-quality hamburger buns
1 cup mixed gourmet salad greens
1 small red onion, sliced thinly
3 tbsp. drained sliced sun-dried tomatoes

Combine beef, breadcrumbs, parsley and two rounded tablespoons of paste in large bowl; shape mixture by hand into four patties.

Heat oil in large skillet; cook patties until browned on both sides and cooked as desired. Place patties on baking sheet; top with mozzarella, place under hot broiler until cheese melts.

Meanwhile, combine remaining paste and mayonnaise in small bowl. Split buns in half, toast cut sides.

Sandwich patties, mayonnaise mixture, lettuce, onion and sliced sun-dried tomatoes between buns.

SERVES 4

per serving: 40.2g fat; 776 calories
tips: Patties can be prepared a day ahead; cover, refrigerate. Cooked patties can be frozen for up to two months.

Steaks with Crunchy Salsa

preparation time 25 minutes

cooking time 10 minutes

4 small beef tenderloin steaks ($1^{1}/4$ lbs.)

CRUNCHY SALSA
1 small red bell pepper, chopped finely
1 small green bell pepper, chopped finely
1 medium red onion, chopped finely
1 large tomato, seeded, chopped finely
$1^{1}/2$ tbsp. chopped fresh cilantro
$^{1}/4$ cup fat-free Italian dressing
2 cloves garlic, crushed
1 tsp. ground cumin

Combine ingredients for crunchy salsa in medium bowl.

Cook beef on heated oiled grill or grill pan until browned on both sides and cooked as desired. Serve with crunchy salsa.

SERVES 4

per serving: 7.5g fat; 244 calories
tip: Salsa can be made several hours ahead; cover, refrigerate.

Beef with Red Wine Sauce and Polenta

preparation time 5 minutes

cooking time 15 minutes

4 small beef tenderloin steaks (1$^1/_4$ lbs.)
$^3/_4$ cup dry red wine
$^1/_3$ cup raspberry preserves
4 cups chicken stock
1$^1/_2$ cups polenta
$^1/_2$ cup (2 oz.) freshly grated parmesan cheese

Heat oiled large skillet; cook steaks until browned on both sides and cooked as desired. Remove from skillet; cover to keep warm.

Add wine and preserves to same skillet; cook, stirring, until sauce thickens slightly. Cover sauce to keep warm.

Meanwhile, bring stock to boil in large pot, add polenta; simmer, stirring, five minutes or until polenta thickens. Stir in cheese.

Serve beef with red wine sauce and polenta.

SERVES 4

per serving: 12.7g fat; 569 calories
tip: This recipe is best made close to serving time.

Pork
& Veal

Pork with Mushrooms, Ginger and Bok Choy

preparation time 10 minutes
(plus standing time)

cooking time 10 minutes

8 dried shiitake mushrooms
$1^{1}/_{2}$ tbsp. peanut oil
3 tsp. grated fresh ginger
1 lb. boneless pork chops, sliced thinly
5 oz. oyster mushrooms
5 oz. button mushrooms, halved
$1^{1}/_{2}$ tbsp. hoisin sauce
1 tsp. cornstarch
$^{1}/_{2}$ cup chicken stock
8 oz. bok choy, chopped roughly

Place mushrooms in small heatproof bowl, cover with boiling water; let stand 20 minutes, drain. Discard stems, slice caps finely.

Heat oil in large skillet; cook ginger until fragrant. Add pork; cook, in batches, until tender. Remove from skillet.

Add all mushrooms to same skillet, cook until hot. Return pork to skillet with sauce and blended cornstarch and stock; stir until sauce boils and thickens slightly. Add bok choy; cook until just wilted.

SERVES **4**

per serving: 7.9g fat; 213 calories
tip: This recipe is best made close to serving time.

Veal Marsala

preparation time 10 minutes

cooking time 15 minutes

8 pieces veal scaloppine (1$^3/_4$ lbs.)
flour for dredging
3 tbsp. vegetable oil
1$^1/_2$ tbsp. butter
$^1/_3$ cup Marsala wine
$^3/_4$ cup heavy cream
$^1/_2$ tsp. cracked black peppercorns
3 tbsp. chopped fresh chives

Toss veal in flour; shake off excess. Heat oil and butter in large skillet; cook veal, in batches, until browned on both sides and cooked as desired. Remove veal from skillet, cover to keep warm. Drain fat from skillet.

Add remaining ingredients to same skillet; simmer, stirring, until sauce thickens slightly.

Return veal and any juices to skillet, coat with sauce; serve immediately with your favorite vegetables.

SERVES 4

per serving: 37.8g fat; 569 calories
tip: This recipe is best made close to serving time.

Gingered Pork with Vegetables

preparation time 10 minutes

cooking time 15 minutes

3 tbsp. grated fresh ginger
$1/4$ cup chopped fresh cilantro
3 tbsp. rice vinegar
$1^{1}/2$ lbs. pork chops, sliced thinly
3 tbsp. peanut oil
4 oz. fresh baby corn, halved lengthwise
1 medium red bell pepper, sliced thinly
$3^{1}/2$ oz. snow peas, halved
3 tbsp. light soy sauce
8 oz. spinach, trimmed
3 cups bean sprouts
$1/2$ cup fresh cilantro, extra

Combine ginger, cilantro and vinegar in medium bowl; toss pork to coat in marinade.

Heat half the oil in large skillet; cook pork mixture, in batches, until pork is browned and cooked through. Remove from skillet.

Heat remaining oil in same skillet; cook corn, bell pepper and peas until just tender. Remove from skillet.

Return pork to skillet with sauce; cook until heated through. Gently toss cooked vegetables with pork, spinach, sprouts and extra cilantro until spinach just wilts.

SERVES 4

per serving: 13.8g fat; 344 calories
tip: This recipe is best made close to serving time.

Ginger Veal Stir-fry

preparation time 10 minutes

cooking time 15 minutes

$1/4$ cup peanut oil
4 veal steaks (1 lb.), sliced
2 medium zucchini, sliced
$3^{1}/_{2}$ oz. snow peas
$3^{1}/_{2}$ oz. green beans
1 medium red bell pepper, chopped
$2/_{3}$ cup pitted prunes
$1/4$ cup dry sherry
1 tsp. soy sauce
2 tsp. lime juice
$1/_{2}$ tsp. ground ginger
$1^{1}/_{2}$ tbsp. sugar
2 scant tbsp. cornstarch
$1/4$ cup water

Heat three tablespoons of oil in large skillet; cook veal until browned all over. Remove from skillet, cover to keep warm.

Add remaining oil to same skillet, add vegetables and prunes; cook until vegetables are just tender. Stir in sherry, soy sauce, lime juice, ginger, sugar and blended cornstarch and water; stir until mixture boils and thickens.

Return veal to skillet, stir until heated through. Serve with rice or noodles, if desired.

SERVES 4

per serving: 17.2g fat; 387 calories
tip: This recipe is best made close to serving time.

Veal Cutlets with Roasted Tomatoes and Spinach Salad

preparation time 15 minutes

cooking time 35 minutes

9 small plum tomatoes (about 1 lb.), halved
$1/4$ cup olive oil
4 oz. green beans
6 veal chops ($1^3/4$ lbs.)
$1/4$ cup small basil leaves
$3^1/2$ cups baby spinach leaves
1 small red onion, sliced thinly
5 tbsp. butter

GARLIC DRESSING
$1/2$ cup olive oil
3 tbsp. balsamic vinegar
3 cloves garlic, crushed
1 tsp. hot mustard

Preheat oven to 425°F. Grease baking dish.

Place tomatoes in prepared dish; drizzle with $1^1/2$ tablespoons of the oil. Cook for 30 minutes or until soft. Meanwhile, place beans in heatproof bowl, cover with boiling water, let stand two minutes; drain. Rinse under cold water. Combine beans, basil, spinach and onion in large bowl.

Heat butter and remaining oil in large skillet; cook chops until browned on both sides and cooked as desired.

Whisk together ingredients for garlic dressing. Add dressing to spinach salad; toss to combine. Serve chops with salad and tomatoes.

SERVES 6

per serving: 21.9g fat; 307 calories
tips: The dressing can be made a day ahead; cover, refrigerate. This recipe is best made just before serving.

Pasta

Veal and Fettuccine with Mustard Cream Sauce

preparation time 10 minutes

cooking time 25 minutes

1/4 cup olive oil
1 medium onion, sliced
1 3/4 lbs. veal shank
flour for dredging
1/2 cup buttermilk
3/4 cup heavy cream
1/2 cup dry white wine
3 tbsp. yellow mustard
1 lb. fresh plain and spinach fettuccine

Heat 1 1/2 tablespoons of the oil in skillet, add onion; cook, stirring, until soft. Remove from skillet; place in large bowl.

Remove meat from shank; cut meat into strips. Toss meat in flour, shake away excess. Heat remaining oil in same skillet, add meat; cook, stirring, until well browned and tender. Remove from skillet; combine with onion.

Boil any juices remaining in skillet on high heat for one minute or until reduced to about 1 1/2 tablespoons. Add buttermilk; stir over medium heat until mixture thickens slightly. Stir in cream, wine and mustard, stirring until mixture boils; simmer, uncovered, until slightly thickened.

Meanwhile, cook pasta in large pot of boiling salted water, uncovered, until just tender; drain, keep warm. Add veal and onion to mustard sauce, stir until heated through; serve over pasta.

SERVES 4

per serving: 37.1g fat; 897 calories
tip: This recipe is best made close to serving time.

Fettuccine Carbonara

preparation time 10 minutes

cooking time 15 minutes

8 oz. dried fettuccine
2 tbsp. softened butter
7 slices bacon or pancetta (Italian-cured bacon)
1/3 cup heavy cream
pinch sweet paprika
1 egg
1 egg yolk, extra
1/2 cup (2 oz.) freshly grated parmesan cheese

Cook pasta in large pot of boiling salted water, uncovered, until just tender; drain. Return pasta to pot with butter, toss over low heat until combined.

Meanwhile, cut bacon into thin strips. Place bacon in large skillet over low heat, cook gently until crisp. Drain fat from skillet, leaving about three tablespoons. Add cream and paprika; stir until combined.

Place egg, egg yolk and half the cheese in bowl; beat until combined.

Add cream mixture, egg mixture and bacon to pasta; toss to combine. Season with freshly ground black pepper; sprinkle with remaining cheese.

SERVES 4

per serving: 24.4g fat; 479 calories
tip: This recipe is best made close to serving time.

Bow-ties with Broccoli and Parmesan

preparation time 20 minutes

cooking time 10 minutes

1 lb. bow-tie pasta (farfalle)
1$^{1}/_{2}$ cups buttermilk
1 clove garlic, crushed
1$^{1}/_{2}$ tbsp. Dijon mustard
$^{1}/_{4}$ cup olive oil
15 oz. broccoli, chopped
$^{1}/_{2}$ cup (2 oz.) sliced almonds, toasted
$^{1}/_{2}$ cup (2 oz.) freshly grated parmesan cheese
6 scallions, sliced finely
3 oz. bean sprouts

Cook pasta in large pot of boiling salted water, uncovered, until just tender; drain.

Meanwhile, whisk buttermilk, garlic, mustard and oil in small bowl until combined.

Boil, steam or microwave broccoli until tender.

Combine hot pasta, buttermilk mixture, broccoli, nuts, cheese and scallions. Stir through and serve with sprouts.

SERVES 4

per serving: 26.3g fat; 750 calories
tip: This recipe is best made close to serving time.

Spaghetti with Chicken and Red Pesto

preparation time 10 minutes

cooking time 20 minutes

4 boneless, skinless chicken breasts (1^1/$_2$ lbs.)
^{1}/$_4$ cup bottled red pesto
12 oz. spaghetti
1 cup stale breadcrumbs
^{1}/$_3$ cup finely chopped fresh chives
2 tsp. whole-grain mustard
^{1}/$_2$ cup chicken stock

We used sun-dried red pepper pesto for this recipe, but any bottled 'red' pesto, such as tomato, could be used.

Coat chicken with half the pesto. Cook chicken on grill or grill pan until browned on both sides and cooked through; cover to keep warm.

Meanwhile, cook spaghetti in large pot of boiling water, uncovered, until just tender; drain. Rinse under cold water; drain.

Heat large oiled pot or skillet; cook breadcrumbs, stirring, until browned. Stir in spaghetti with remaining pesto, chives, mustard and stock; cook, stirring, until hot.

Serve spaghetti with sliced chicken and tomato wedges, if desired.

SERVES 4

per serving: 15.7g fat; 671 calories
tip: This recipe is best made close to serving time.

Mediterranean Tortellini

preparation time 10 minutes

cooking time 15 minutes

2 medium red bell peppers
1 1/2 tbsp. olive oil
2 cloves garlic, crushed
1 serrano chile, seeded, sliced
4 large plum tomatoes, chopped
6 artichoke hearts in oil, quartered
1/2 cup black olives, seeded, sliced
1 1/2 tbsp. fresh oregano
1 3/4 lbs. cheese and spinach tortellini

Quarter bell peppers; discard seeds and membranes. Roast under broiler, skin-side up, until skin blisters and blackens. Cover bell pepper pieces with plastic wrap or aluminum foil for five minutes; peel away skin, slice peppers thickly.

Heat oil in large skillet; cook garlic and chile, stirring, until fragrant. Add bell peppers, tomatoes and artichokes; cook, stirring, until hot. Stir in olives and oregano.

Meanwhile, cook tortellini in large pot of boiling salted water, uncovered, until just tender; drain. Serve sauce over tortellini.

SERVES 6

per serving: 15.3g fat; 290 calories
tip: Sauce can be made a day ahead; cover, refrigerate.

Fettuccine with Italian Sausage and Olives

preparation time 10 minutes

cooking time 25 minutes

1 lb. fresh fettuccine pasta
1 lb. Italian-style pork sausages
3 tbsp. olive oil
5 oz. button mushrooms, sliced
2 cloves garlic, crushed
$2/3$ cup large green olives, seeded, sliced
1 tsp. grated lemon peel
$1^1/2$ tbsp. lemon juice
3 tbsp. chopped fresh flat-leaf parsley
$1^1/2$ cups heavy cream

Cook pasta in large pot of boiling salted water, uncovered, until just tender; drain.

Cook sausages in dry skillet over medium heat, turning regularly, 10 minutes or until browned and cooked through; drain on paper towels. Cut sausages into $1/2$-inch slices.

Heat oil in same skillet, add mushrooms and garlic; cook, stirring, two minutes or until mushrooms are soft. Stir in sausages, olives, lemon peel and juice, parsley and cream; simmer, stirring occasionally, 10 minutes or until reduced by $1/3$.

Add pasta to skillet; cook, stirring, three minutes or until pasta is heated through.

SERVES 4

per serving: 70.4g fat; 888 calories
tip: Sausages can be cooked a day ahead; cover, refrigerate.

Spaghetti with Smoked Salmon

preparation time 15 minutes

cooking time 15 minutes

1 lb. spaghetti
3 tbsp. olive oil
1 medium onion, chopped
14 oz. sliced smoked salmon, cut into $3/4$" strips
1 lb. fresh asparagus, halved
$1^1/_2$ tbsp. brandy
2 tsp. mustard seeds
3 cups heavy cream
3 tbsp. shredded fresh basil

Cook pasta in large pot of boiling salted water, uncovered, until just tender; drain.

Heat oil in skillet; cook onion, stirring, until soft. Add salmon, asparagus, brandy, seeds and cream. Bring to a boil, simmer, uncovered, until slightly thickened; stir in basil.

Stir sauce through pasta.

SERVES 4

per serving: 80.3g fat; 1,287 calories
tip: This recipe is best made just before serving time.

Roman Tomato Soup

preparation time 10 minutes

cooking time 15 minutes

$1^{1}/_{2}$ tbsp. olive oil
2 cloves garlic, crushed
1 medium onion, chopped finely
16-oz. can condensed tomato soup
14-oz. can crushed tomatoes, undrained
3 cups water
2 cups small fusilli (spiral pasta)
$1^{1}/_{2}$ tbsp. finely chopped fresh basil
3 slices bacon, chopped finely

Heat oil in large skillet; cook garlic and onion, stirring, until onion is soft. Add undiluted soup, tomatoes, water and pasta. Bring to boil; simmer, uncovered, about 10 minutes or until pasta is just tender. Stir in basil.

Meanwhile, cook bacon in medium heated oiled skillet until browned and crisp; drain on paper towels. Ladle soup into serving bowls; sprinkle with bacon.

SERVES 4

per serving: 6.1g fat; 310 calories
tips: This recipe can be made two days ahead; cover, refrigerate. Soup can also be frozen for up to two months.

Angel-hair Pasta with Chili

preparation time 10 minutes

cooking time 15 minutes

1 lb. fresh angel-hair pasta
1/2 cup olive oil
2 serrano chiles, seeded, chopped finely
4 cloves garlic, crushed
1 cup finely chopped fresh cilantro
2 tsp. salt
3 tbsp. lemon juice
3/4 cup (3 oz.) freshly shaved parmesan cheese

We used fresh angel-hair pasta here,
but any fine pasta, such as vermicelli,
can be substituted.

Cook pasta in large pot of boiling salted water, uncovered, until just tender; drain.

Meanwhile, heat oil in large skillet; cook chile and garlic, stirring, three minutes or until fragrant. Remove skillet from heat; stir in cilantro and salt.

Gently toss cilantro mixture with pasta and lemon juice in skillet. Just before serving, sprinkle with cheese.

SERVES 4

per serving: 34.8g fat; 740 calories
tip: This recipe is best made close to serving time.

Spiced Beef Pasta Salad

preparation time 10 minutes
(plus cooling time)

cooking time 25 minutes

$1^{1}/_{2}$ tbsp. vegetable oil
1 lb. ground beef
1 tsp. ground coriander
1 tsp. ground cumin
$^{1}/_{4}$ tsp. chili powder
$^{1}/_{2}$ tsp. sweet paprika
1 medium red bell pepper
1 medium yellow bell pepper
5 oz. green beans, chopped

8 oz. penne pasta
2 tsp. chopped fresh cilantro

DRESSING
3 tbsp. light soy sauce
$^{1}/_{4}$ cup dry sherry
$1^{1}/_{2}$ tbsp. mirin
$1^{1}/_{2}$ tbsp. honey
3 tbsp. tomato sauce

Heat oil in skillet; cook beef and spices, stirring, until beef is browned. Remove from heat; cool.

Quarter bell peppers; discard seeds and membranes. Roast under broiler, skin-side up, until skin blisters and blackens. Cover bell pepper pieces with plastic wrap or aluminum foil for five minutes; peel away skin, cut bell peppers into strips.

Boil, steam or microwave beans until just tender, rinse under cold water; drain. Combine beef mixture, bell peppers and beans in large bowl. Meanwhile, cook pasta in large pot of boiling salted water, uncovered, until just tender; drain.

Whisk together ingredients for dressing. Add to beef mixture with pasta and cilantro; toss to combine.

SERVES 4

per serving: 17.2g fat; 528 calories
tip: Salad can be made three hours ahead; cover, refrigerate.

Mushroom Trio with Ravioli

preparation time 10 minutes

cooking time 15 minutes

1$\frac{3}{4}$ lbs. fresh beef ravioli
1 tsp. olive oil
2 cloves garlic, crushed
2 tsp. grated fresh ginger
2 cilantro sprigs, chopped
1 serrano chile, seeded, chopped
8 oz. button mushrooms, quartered
8 oz. cremini mushrooms, halved
1 cup fat-free evaporated milk
7 oz. shiitake mushrooms, quartered
$\frac{1}{4}$ cup fresh cilantro

Cook ravioli in large pot of boiling salted water, uncovered, until tender; drain.

Meanwhile, heat oil in large skillet; cook garlic, ginger, cilantro and chile until fragrant. Add button and cremini mushrooms to skillet; cook, stirring, two minutes. Stir in milk; bring to a boil, stirring occasionally, until milk is slightly thickened. Stir in shiitake mushrooms; cook, stirring, until hot.

Serve mushroom mixture over ravioli; sprinkle with cilantro leaves.

SERVES 4

per serving: 9.2g fat; 379 calories
tip: This recipe is best made close to serving time.

Baked Feta and Roasted Tomato Pasta Salad

preparation time 10 minutes

cooking time 20 minutes

10$^{1}/_{2}$ oz. feta cheese, crumbled
$^{1}/_{2}$ cup olive oil
1 lb. cherry tomatoes
12 oz. penne
$^{1}/_{4}$ cup pine nuts, toasted
$^{1}/_{2}$ cup firmly packed small fresh basil leaves
$^{1}/_{2}$ cup seeded black olives, sliced

We used penne in this salad but use any short pasta you like—try farfalle or fusilli.

Preheat oven to 475°F.

Place cheese on large piece of aluminum foil; bring sides of aluminum up around cheese, drizzle with three tablespoons of the oil. Enclose cheese in aluminum; place at one end of shallow baking dish.

Combine tomatoes with 1$^{1}/_{2}$ tablespoons of the remaining oil in same baking dish. Bake, uncovered, 15 minutes or until tomatoes are soft.

Meanwhile, cook pasta in large pot of boiling salted water, uncovered, until just tender; drain.

Combine pasta with tomatoes, cheese and any pan juices in large bowl with remaining oil, pine nuts, basil and olives.

SERVES **4**

per serving: 54.3g fat; 874 calories
tip: This recipe is best made close to serving time.

Linguini with Pancetta and Tomato Sauce

preparation time 10 minutes

cooking time 20 minutes

1 lb. linguini
1 1/2 tbsp. olive oil
1 large onion, chopped
5 oz. pancetta, chopped
three 15-oz. cans whole tomatoes,
   drained, chopped
1/2 cup pimiento-stuffed green olives, sliced
1/4 cup (1 oz.) grated romano cheese

Cook pasta in large pot of boiling salted water, uncovered, until just tender; drain.

Meanwhile, heat oil in skillet; cook onion and pancetta, stirring, until onion is soft.

Add tomatoes to pan, bring to a boil; reduce heat, simmer, uncovered, 10 minutes or until mixture thickens slightly. Add olives; mix well.

Serve sauce over pasta. Top with romano cheese.

SERVES 6

per serving: 9.6g fat; 407 calories
tips: Sauce can be made a day ahead;
cover, refrigerate. Sauce can also be
frozen for up to two months.

Spaghetti with Seafood and Herbs

preparation time 10 minutes
cooking time 20 minutes

12 oz. spaghetti
2 large carrots
1/3 cup olive oil
1 lb. uncooked peeled shrimp
5 oz. snow peas
1 lb. scallops
2 cloves garlic, crushed
1/3 cup chopped fresh basil
3 tbsp. chopped fresh chives
2 tsp. grated lemon peel
1/3 cup lemon juice
1 tsp. cracked black peppercorns

Cook pasta in large pot of boiling salted water, uncovered, until just tender; drain.

Meanwhile, cut carrots into thin strips.

Heat oil in large skillet; cook shrimp, carrots, snow peas, scallops and garlic until seafood is tender. Add herbs, lemon peel, lemon juice and pepper; stir until well combined. Toss seafood mixture through hot pasta.

SERVES 4

per serving: 21.2g fat; 684 calories
tip: This recipe is best made close to serving time.

Spaghetti with Tuna and Olives

preparation time 10 minutes

cooking time 15 minutes

12 oz. spaghetti
two 6-oz. cans tuna, drained
2 medium tomatoes, chopped
$1/2$ cup seeded black olives, halved
3 tsp. chopped fresh dill
$1/4$ cup Italian salad dressing

Cook pasta in large pot of boiling salted water, uncovered, until just tender, drain.

Return pasta to pot with tuna and remaining ingredients; toss gently over medium heat until warm.

SERVES 4

per serving: 26.3g fat; 647 calories
tips: This recipe is best made close to serving time and served hot. It can also be made several hours ahead and served cold.

Penne Boscaiola

preparation time 10 minutes

cooking time 15 minutes

12 oz. penne pasta
1$^{1}/_{2}$ tbsp. olive oil
1 large onion, chopped finely
3 cloves garlic, crushed
7 slices bacon, chopped finely
5 oz. button mushrooms, chopped
1$^{1}/_{2}$ cups heavy cream
$^{1}/_{2}$ cup (2 oz.) freshly grated parmesan cheese

*The quill-shaped penne is a good pasta to serve
with a rich, substantial sauce like a boscaiola or
carbonara because the ridges on each piece of pasta
help 'trap' the creamy sauce and absorb its flavor.*

Cook pasta in large pot of boiling salted water, uncovered, until just tender; drain.

Meanwhile, heat oil in large skillet; cook onion, garlic, bacon and mushrooms, stirring, until onion is soft and browned lightly. Add cream to skillet; stir until combined.

Add pasta and cheese to skillet; gently toss with mushroom cream sauce until heated through.

SERVES 4

per serving: 42.7g fat; 753 calories
tip: This recipe is best made close to serving time.

Seafood

Salmon Patties

preparation time 25 minutes

cooking time 10 minutes

5 medium potatoes (about 2 lbs.), chopped
15- to 16-oz. can salmon
1 trimmed celery stalk, chopped finely
1 small onion, grated
1 small red bell pepper, chopped finely
$1^1/2$ tbsp. chopped fresh flat-leaf parsley
1 tsp. grated lemon peel
$1^1/2$ tbsp. lemon juice
$^1/2$ cup flour for dredging
1 egg, beaten lightly
3 tbsp. milk
1 cup packaged breadcrumbs
 (plus extra if needed)
1 cup stale breadcrumbs (plus extra if needed)
oil for deep frying

Boil, steam or microwave potatoes until tender; drain well. Place in medium bowl; mash until smooth.

Drain salmon well, remove skin and bones; add to potatoes in bowl, mash with fork. Add celery, onion, bell pepper, parsley, lemon peel and lemon juice; mix well.

Divide salmon mixture into eight portions. Shape each portion into a patty; dust with flour, shake away excess. Brush patties with combined egg and milk, toss in combined breadcrumbs; reshape if necessary while patting on the breadcrumbs.

Deep-fry patties, in batches, in hot oil for two minutes or until golden brown and heated through; drain on paper towels. Serve with lemon wedges.

SERVES 8

per serving: 15.3g fat; 331 calories
tip: Patties can be prepared up to a
day ahead; cover, refrigerate. Deep-fry
just before serving.

Spicy Lemon Seafood Soup

preparation time 15 minutes

cooking time 35 minutes

1 lb. uncooked medium shrimp
8 oz. white fish fillets
7 oz. cleaned calamari
3 tbsp. roughly chopped, fresh
  flat-leaf parsley
1 large red onion, halved, sliced
2 cloves garlic, crushed
2 rounded tbsp. grated lemon peel
3 bay leaves
1 tsp. sweet paprika
2 serrano chiles, sliced
1/2 cup dry white wine

1/4 cup lemon juice
2 tsp. olive oil
2 scallions, chopped

FISH STOCK
3 lbs. fish bones
10 cups water
1 medium onion, chopped
2 trimmed celery stalks,
  chopped coarsely
2 bay leaves
1 tsp. black peppercorns

Make fish stock. Meanwhile, peel and devein shrimp, leaving tails intact. Cut fish and calamari into 3/4-inch pieces.

Heat oil in large pot; cook red onion and garlic, stirring, until onion is soft. Add lemon peel, bay leaves, paprika, chile, wine, lemon juice and stock; simmer, uncovered, 20 minutes. Add seafood, parsley and scallions; simmer, uncovered, two minutes or until seafood is just cooked. Discard bay leaves.

Fish Stock: combine ingredients in large pot; simmer, uncovered, 20 minutes. Strain mixture through cheese cloth-lined strainer into large clean bowl.

SERVES 6

per serving: 4g fat; 186 calories
tip: This recipe is best made just before serving time.

Stir-fried Spicy Fish

preparation time 10 minutes

cooking time 10 minutes

14 oz. boneless white fish fillets
1 tsp. dried thyme
1 tsp. dried parsley flakes
2 tsp. garlic salt
1 tsp. paprika
1 tsp. onion powder
$1/2$ tsp. cracked black peppercorns
$10^1/2$ oz. baby yellow squash, sliced
5 oz. green beans, sliced
$1^1/2$ tbsp. vegetable oil
2 tbsp. butter
few drops Tabasco sauce

Cut fish into $1^1/4$-inch pieces; pat dry with paper towels. Combine herbs and spices in large bowl; add fish, toss to coat in herb mixture.

Boil, steam or microwave squash and beans until just tender, drain immediately; rinse under cold water, drain.

Heat oil in large skillet; cook fish, in batches, until tender. Add squash, beans and butter; cook until hot. Add sauce to taste.

SERVES 4

per serving: 13.5g fat; 233 calories
tip: This recipe is best made close to serving time.

Marinated Tuna Kebabs

preparation time 10 minutes
(plus standing time)

cooking time 10 minutes

2 lbs. fresh tuna

MARINADE
1/2 cup fresh parsley sprigs
1/2 cup fresh cilantro
3 cloves garlic, bruised
1 tsp. ground cinnamon
1 tsp. ground cumin
1 tsp. ground sweet paprika
1 tsp. ground coriander
1/2 cup lemon juice
1/4 cup olive oil
1 tsp. grated lemon peel

Soak bamboo skewers in water for one hour before use to prevent them from splintering and scorching.

Cut tuna into $1^{1}/4$-inch cubes. Blend or process ingredients for marinade until smooth, place in large bowl; add tuna, toss to coat in marinade. Cover; let stand 10 minutes.

Thread tuna onto eight skewers; reserve marinade. Grill or barbecue, brushing with reserved marinade, until cooked as desired, turning once during cooking.

Serve with lemon wedges, if desired.

SERVES 8

per serving: 14.1g fat; 259 calories
tip: This recipe can be prepared a day ahead, cover; refrigerate.

Cajun Fish Fillets with Tomato Cucumber Raita

1$^{1}/_{2}$ tbsp. Cajun seasoning
1$^{1}/_{2}$ tbsp. flour
1 tsp. ground cumin
4 white fish fillets (2 lbs.)
3 tbsp. lemon juice

Cutlets of cod were used in this recipe.

TOMATO CUCUMBER RAITA
2 cups plain yogurt
3 small cucumbers, seeded, chopped finely
2 medium tomatoes, seeded, chopped finely
1$^{1}/_{2}$ tbsp. lemon juice
1 tsp. ground cumin

Raita is a tangy Indian-style sauce of yogurt blended with cucumber.

Combine seasoning, flour and cumin in small bowl; sprinkle over fish. Cook fish on heated oiled grill or grill pan until browned on both sides and cooked as desired.

Combine ingredients for tomato cucumber raita in medium bowl.

Just before serving, drizzle fish with lemon juice; serve with tomato cucumber raita.

SERVES 4

per serving: 6.5g fat; 284 calories
tip: This recipe is best made close to serving time.

Easy Nicoise Salad

preparation time 10 minutes

no cooking time required

4 oz. green beans
five 6-oz. cans tuna, drained
1 large head red-leaf lettuce
14-oz. can new potatoes, drained, quartered
8 oz. cherry tomatoes, halved
1 cup black olives, pitted

DRESSING
$^1/_2$ cup low-fat Italian dressing
2 tsp. whole-grain mustard
1 clove garlic, crushed
2 tsp. fresh chervil

Place beans in medium heatproof bowl, cover with boiling water, let stand five minutes; drain. Rinse beans under cold water; drain well.

Break tuna into large chunks, place in large bowl with beans, tuna, potatoes, tomatoes and olives; toss gently to combine.

Combine ingredients for dressing in small bowl.

Line large serving bowl with lettuce; top with salad, drizzle salad with dressing.

SERVES 6

per serving: 16.3g fat; 332 calories
tips: Salad mixture can be prepared three hours ahead; cover, refrigerate. Add salad mixture to lettuce-lined bowl and add dressing just before serving.

Spicy Tomato Shrimp

preparation time 15 minutes

cooking time 10 minutes

2 lbs. uncooked medium shrimp
2 tsp. hot paprika
1 tsp. coriander seeds, crushed
1 tsp. ground turmeric
1 tsp. ground cumin
1 tsp. cracked black pepper
$^1/_4$ tsp. ground cloves
$^1/_4$ tsp. ground cardamom
$^1/_4$ cup water
1$^1/_2$ tbsp. light olive oil
2 medium onions, sliced
2 large tomatoes (about 1 lb.), chopped
3 tbsp. finely chopped fresh cilantro

Peel and devein shrimp, leaving tails intact. Combine spices and water in small bowl.

Heat oil in skillet; add onions, cook, stirring, two minutes. Add spice mixture, cook, stirring, until fragrant.

Add shrimp and tomatoes; cook, stirring, until shrimp have changed in color and are just tender. Remove from heat; stir in fresh cilantro.

SERVES 4

per serving: 5.7g fat; 198 calories
tip: This recipe is best made close to serving time.

Tuna, Bean and Grilled Vegetable Salad

preparation time 25 minutes

cooking time 10 minutes

1 medium red bell pepper
1 medium yellow bell pepper
1 large onion
4 large zucchini (about $1^{1}/4$ lbs.)
$1/3$ cup olive oil
7 oz. button mushrooms, halved
14-oz. can cannellini beans, drained, rinsed
15 oz. canned tuna, drained, flaked
$1/4$ cup lemon juice
1 clove garlic, crushed
$1^{1}/2$ tbsp. finely chopped, fresh flat-leaf parsley

Quarter bell peppers; discard seeds and membranes. Roast under broiler, skin-side up, until skin blisters and blackens. Cover bell pepper pieces with plastic wrap or aluminum foil for five minutes; peel away skin, then cut peppers into thick strips.

Cut onion into eight wedges; cut zucchini diagonally into $1/2$-inch slices. Place onion and zucchini on baking sheet, brush with $1^{1}/2$ tablespoons of the oil; cook under broiler until browned lightly on both sides.

Heat $1^{1}/2$ tablespoons of the oil in small skillet; cook mushrooms, stirring, until browned lightly.

Combine bell peppers, onion, zucchini, mushrooms, beans and tuna in large bowl; gently toss with combined remaining oil, lemon juice, garlic and parsley.

SERVES 4

per serving: 31.2g fat; 471 calories
tip: Vegetables can be cooked up to two days ahead; cover, refrigerate. Reheat or bring to room temperature before adding to tuna.

Pan-fried Fish with White Wine Sauce

preparation time 5 minutes

cooking time 25 minutes

1¹/₂ tbsp. butter
1 medium white onion, chopped finely
¹/₃ cup dry white wine
¹/₂ cup heavy cream
1¹/₂ tbsp. coarsely chopped fresh chervil or
  flat-leaf parsley
4 small fish fillets (1³/₄ lbs.)

We used snapper fillets for this recipe.

Melt butter in small pot; cook onion, stirring, until soft. Add wine; simmer, uncovered, until wine is almost evaporated. Add cream; simmer, uncovered, until sauce thickens slightly. Stir in chervil or parsley just before serving.

Meanwhile, heat large oiled skillet; cook fish until browned on both sides and cooked through.

Just before serving, stir chervil or parsley through sauce; serve fish and sauce with roasted potato wedges, if desired.

SERVES 4

per serving: 22.2g fat; 393 calories
tip: This recipe is best made close to serving time.

Salt and Pepper Butterflied Shrimp

preparation time 30 minutes

cooking time 10 minutes

four 3 1/2-inch square wonton wrappers
2 lbs. uncooked medium shrimp
vegetable oil for frying
1 1/2 tbsp. peanut oil
2 cloves garlic, crushed
1 serrano chile, sliced
2 tsp. sesame seeds, toasted
3 tbsp. mild sweet Thai chili sauce

3 scallions, sliced thinly
1 1/2 tbsp. lime juice

SEASONING
1/2 tsp. black peppercorns
1/4 tsp. coriander seeds
3/4 tsp. sea salt flakes
1/4 tsp. lemon pepper

Cut wonton wrappers in half diagonally. Peel shrimp, leaving tails intact. Cut shrimp down the back, cutting nearly all the way through; remove veins, flatten shrimp slightly.

Fry wonton wrappers in hot oil, in batches, until lightly browned; drain on paper towels.

Fry shrimp in hot oil, in batches, about 30 seconds or until shrimp are almost tender and have changed color; drain on paper towels. Combine ingredients for seasoning in small bowl.

Heat peanut oil in large skillet; cook garlic and chile until fragrant. Add shrimp, lime juice, chili sauce and seasoning; cook until heated through. Stir in scallions, sprinkle with sesame seeds. Serve with wonton wrappers.

Seasoning: lightly crush peppercorns and coriander seeds; combine with salt and lemon pepper.

SERVES 4

per serving: 6.5g fat; 163 calories
tip: This recipe is best made just before serving time.

Shrimp with Garlic Herb Butter

preparation time 15 minutes

cooking time 10 minutes

2 lbs. uncooked medium shrimp
3 tbsp. olive oil
6 cloves garlic, crushed
4 tbsp. butter, chopped
$1^{1}/_{2}$ tbsp. lemon juice
2 heaping tbsp. chopped fresh flat-leaf parsley

Peel and devein shrimp, leaving tails intact.

Heat oil in large skillet; cook garlic, stirring, until soft. Add shrimp; cook, turning gently, until shrimp start to change color and are almost cooked.

Add butter and lemon juice to skillet; cook, until shrimp are just cooked through. Stir in parsley.

SERVES 6

per serving: 13.5g; 192 calories
tip: This recipe is best made just before serving time.

Tuna and Braised Onion Salad

preparation time 10 minutes

cooking time 30 minutes

$^1/_4$ cup olive oil
2 tbsp. butter
3 large onions (about 1$^1/_4$ lbs.), sliced
3 tbsp. red wine vinegar
4 tuna steaks (about 1$^1/_4$ lbs.)
3 cups arugula
12 oz. spinach, shredded

Heat oil and butter in heavy-based skillet, add onions; cook, covered, stirring occasionally, about 20 minutes or until onions are very soft. Add vinegar; simmer, uncovered, one minute.

Add tuna to same skillet; cook, uncovered, until tuna is cooked as desired. Remove from skillet; cut into pieces.

Serve warm tuna with braised onions, arugula and spinach.

SERVES 4

per serving: 29g fat; 473 calories
tip: Onions can be cooked up to three days ahead; cover, refrigerate. Cook tuna close to serving time.

Vegetarian

Red Lentils and Artichokes with Capers

preparation time 15 minutes

cooking time 15 minutes

1$^{1}/_{2}$ cups red lentils
$^{1}/_{4}$ cup olive oil
2 medium red onions, sliced
two 14-oz. cans artichoke hearts,
  drained, halved
2 cloves garlic, crushed
3 tbsp. drained capers, finely chopped
3 tbsp. chopped fresh parsley
$^{1}/_{4}$ cup seedless black olives, finely chopped
2 large tomatoes (about 1 lb.), chopped
$^{1}/_{2}$ cup water
$^{1}/_{4}$ cup tomato paste
1$^{1}/_{2}$ tbsp. red wine vinegar
2 tsp. sugar

Cook lentils in large pot of boiling water, uncovered, about eight minutes or until just tender; drain. Rinse; drain.

Heat half the oil in large skillet; cook onions, stirring, until just soft.

Add remaining oil to skillet with artichokes, garlic, capers, parsley, olives and tomatoes; cook, stirring, until combined. Add lentils and remaining ingredients; stir until hot.

SERVES 4

per serving: 16g fat; 411 calories
tip: This recipe can be made a day ahead; cover, refrigerate.

Vegetable Soup with Pesto

preparation time 10 minutes

cooking time 35 minutes

1 small leek, chopped finely
2 medium carrots, chopped finely
1 small potato, chopped finely
1 small onion, chopped finely
1 small zucchini chopped finely
1 small tomato, chopped finely
4 cups vegetable stock
$1/4$ cup macaroni
$10 1/2$-oz. can cannellini or other white beans,
  rinsed, drained

PESTO
$1/4$ cup (1 oz.) freshly grated parmesan cheese
$1/4$ cup chopped fresh basil
2 cloves garlic
$1/4$ cup olive oil

Combine leek, carrots, potato, onion, zucchini, tomato and stock in large pot. Bring to a boil; simmer, covered, 20 minutes or until vegetables are tender.

Add macaroni to pot; simmer, covered, 10 minutes. Add cannellini beans; simmer, uncovered, five minutes or until heated through.

Meanwhile, blend or process ingredients for pesto until smooth. Just before serving, drop spoonfuls of pesto into hot soup.

SERVES 4

per serving: 16.8g fat; 269 calories
tip: This recipe can be made a day ahead; cover soup and pesto separately, refrigerate.

Roasted Vegetable Salad

preparation time 15 minutes

cooking time 20 minutes

3 medium red bell peppers (about $1^{1}/_{4}$ lbs.)
2 lbs. Italian eggplants
$^{1}/_{3}$ cup olive oil
$^{1}/_{3}$ cup chopped pistachios, toasted

YOGURT DRESSING
1 cup plain yogurt
1 clove garlic, crushed
$^{1}/_{4}$ cup chopped fresh cilantro
$1^{1}/_{3}$ tbsp. chopped fresh oregano
1 tsp. ground cumin
2 tsp. honey

Quarter bell peppers; discard seeds and membranes. Roast under broiler, skin-side up, until skin blisters and blackens. Cover bell pepper pieces with plastic wrap or aluminum for five minutes; peel away skin, then slice peppers thickly.

Cut eggplants in half lengthwise. Heat $1^{1}/_{2}$ tablespoons of the oil in skillet, add a quarter of the eggplants to skillet; cook 10 minutes or until browned all over and very soft; drain on paper towels. Repeat with remaining oil and eggplants.

Combine ingredients for yogurt dressing in small bowl; mix well. Spread $^{1}/_{4}$ of the yogurt dressing onto large serving plate; top with $^{1}/_{3}$ of the eggplants, then $^{1}/_{3}$ of the bell peppers. Repeat layering twice more. Top with remaining yogurt dressing; sprinkle with nuts.

SERVES 6

per serving: 18.5g fat; 245 calories
tip: Bell peppers, eggplants and yogurt dressing can be prepared a day ahead; cover separately, refrigerate. Bring to room temperature before serving.

Garbanzo and Rosemary Soup

preparation time 5 minutes

cooking time 15 minutes

3 tbsp. olive oil
8 spring onions, sliced
2 cloves garlic, crushed
3 tbsp. chopped fresh rosemary
15-oz. can crushed tomatoes, undrained
3 cups beef stock
$10^1/_2$-oz. can garbanzos, drained

Heat oil in large pot; add onions, garlic and rosemary; cook, stirring, until onions are soft.

Stir in tomatoes; cook, stirring, five minutes. Add stock and garbanzos; simmer, uncovered, five minutes or until heated through.

SERVES 4

per serving: 10.8g fat; 176 calories
tip: This recipe can be made a day ahead; cover, refrigerate.

Tomato, Feta and Spinach Cakes

preparation time 15 minutes

cooking time 15 minutes

8 oz. frozen spinach, thawed
1 sheet ready-rolled puff pastry
1/3 cup bottled pesto
7 oz. feta cheese, crumbled
1/4 cup finely chopped fresh basil
8 oz. cherry tomatoes, halved
1/4 cup (1 oz.) freshly grated parmesan cheese
1 tsp. cracked black pepper

Preheat oven to 475°F. Grease two baking sheets.

Drain spinach, then squeeze excess liquid from spinach by hand; chop roughly.

Place 1/2 sheet of pastry on each prepared baking sheet. Fold edges of pastry inward to form 1/2-inch border; pinch corners of crusts together.

Divide pesto between crusts; spread evenly to cover crust. Top each with spinach, feta, basil and tomatoes; sprinkle with parmesan and pepper. Bake 15 minutes or until crisp and browned lightly.

SERVES 4

per serving: 31.4g fat; 383 calories
tip: This recipe is best made close to serving time.

Char-grilled Vegetables in Mint Vinaigrette

preparation time 20 minutes

cooking time 15 minutes

3 medium red bell peppers (1^1/4 lbs.)
3 medium green zucchini
3 medium yellow squash
4 baby eggplants
3 tbsp. olive oil
8 oz. cherry tomatoes, halved

MINT VINAIGRETTE
2 cloves garlic, crushed
2 tsp. cumin seeds, toasted
^{1}/2 cup olive oil
1^1/2 tbsp. lemon juice
3 tbsp. red wine vinegar
1^1/2 tbsp. shredded fresh mint

Quarter bell peppers; discard seeds and membranes. Roast under broiler, skin-side up, until skin blisters and blackens. Cover bell pepper pieces with plastic wrap or aluminum foil for five minutes; peel away skin, then slice peppers thickly.

Cut zucchini and eggplants lengthwise into ^{1}/2-inch slices. Heat oil on grill or grill pan, cook zucchini and eggplants, in batches, until charred and cooked through; remove from pan. Cook tomatoes on same grill pan until just softened.

Whisk together ingredients for mint vinaigrette. Arrange vegetables on a plate, drizzle with mint vinaigrette; serve immediately.

SERVES 4

per serving: 38.7g fat; 413 calories
tips: Vegetables are best cooked just before serving time. Mint vinaigrette can be made a day ahead; cover, refrigerate.

Pesto Pizzas

preparation time 20 minutes

cooking time 20 minutes

cooking-oil spray
$1/2$ cup pumpkin seeds
$1/4$ cup firmly packed fresh basil
$1/4$ cup firmly packed fresh parsley
1 clove garlic, crushed
$1/4$ cup tomato puree
1 small sweet potato
5 oz. button mushrooms, sliced
$1/2$ cup (2 oz.) shredded low-fat cheddar cheese
$1/2$ cup (2 oz.) shredded low-fat mozzarella cheese
$1/2$ cup (2 oz.) freshly grated parmesan cheese
4 small fresh or frozen pizza crusts
  (whole-wheat or plain)

Preheat oven to 400°F. Coat two baking sheets with cooking-oil spray.

Cook pumpkin seeds in dry skillet, stirring, over low heat about five minutes or until seeds have popped; cool.

Process pumpkin seeds, herbs and garlic until combined. Gradually add puree while motor is running.

Using a vegetable peeler, cut sweet potato into ribbons.

Place pizza crusts on prepared baking sheets. Divide pumpkin-seed pesto among crusts, top with sweet potato and mushrooms; sprinkle with combined cheeses. Bake 20 minutes or until browned and crisp.

SERVES 4

per serving: 26.3g fat; 1,083 calories
tip: This recipe best made close to serving time.

Leek and Pumpkin Phyllo Pockets

preparation time 20 minutes

cooking time 25 minutes

1 $3/4$ lbs. pumpkin, chopped
2 tbsp. butter
2 medium leeks (about 1 $1/2$ lbs.),
 chopped coarsely
$3/4$ cup (3 oz.) shredded cheddar cheese
3 tbsp. whole-grain mustard
13-oz. package phyllo pastry
$2/3$ cup vegetable oil

Preheat oven to 400°F. Grease baking sheet.

Boil, steam or microwave pumpkin until just tender; drain. Meanwhile, heat butter in medium skillet; cook leeks, stirring, until soft. Combine leeks and pumpkin in large bowl with cheese and mustard; mix well.

To prevent phyllo from drying out, cover sheets with parchment paper and a damp dish towel until ready to use. Working with three sheets at a time, brush each sheet lightly with oil; fold in half. Place $1/2$ cup of vegetable mixture at one end of folded phyllo; roll to enclose filling, folding in sides of phyllo as you roll. Repeat with remaining vegetable mixture and phyllo.

Place phyllo pockets on prepared tray; brush lightly with oil. Bake, uncovered, about 20 minutes or until pastry is browned lightly. Serve with salad, if desired.

SERVES 8

per serving: 27g fat; 418 calories
tips: Pumpkin filling can be made two days ahead; cover, refrigerate. Pumpkin can be substituted with sweet potato if out of season.

Lentil and Vegetable Curry

preparation time 10 minutes

cooking time 30 minutes

1$^1/_2$ cups red lentils
1$^1/_2$ tbsp. vegetable oil
1 large onion, chopped coarsely
2 cloves garlic, crushed
3 tsp. mustard seeds
2 tsp. cumin seeds
2 tsp. ground turmeric
14-oz. can crushed tomatoes, undrained
3 cups vegetable stock
3 medium carrots, chopped coarsely
1 medium potato, chopped coarsely
$^1/_2$ cup coconut milk
$^1/_2$ cup frozen peas

Rinse lentils; drain.

Heat oil in large pot; cook onion and garlic, stirring, until onion is soft. Add seeds and turmeric; cook, stirring, until seeds start to pop. Add tomatoes, stock, carrots, potato and lentils; simmer, covered, 20 minutes or until vegetables and lentils are just tender.

Just before serving, add milk and peas; stir over low heat until just hot.

SERVES 4

per serving: 14.5g fat; 418 calories
tips: Vegetables and lentils can be cooked a day ahead; cover, refrigerate. Reheat and add coconut milk and peas just before serving time.

Gazpacho Celery Salad

preparation time 15 minutes

cooking time 10 minutes

$1/3$ cup red lentils
1 small cucumber
3 cups arugula
1 cup walnuts, toasted
10 celery stalks (about $1^3/4$ lbs.),
  trimmed, sliced finely
12 oz. grape tomatoes,
  halved

GAZPACHO DRESSING
$1/2$ cup tomato juice
$1^1/2$ tbsp. olive oil
$1^1/2$ tbsp. chopped fresh dill
1 clove garlic, crushed
1 tsp. sugar
1 tsp. red wine vinegar
$1/2$ tsp. Tabasco sauce

You need a large bunch of celery (about 2 lbs.) for this recipe.

Rinse lentils under cold water; drain. Cook lentils in small pot of boiling water, uncovered, about five minutes or until just tender; drain, cool.

Whisk together ingredients for gazpacho dressing.

Halve cucumber lengthwise, then slice finely. Combine lentils and cucumber slices with remaining ingredients in large bowl; gently toss with gazpacho dressing.

SERVES 6

per serving: 15.2kg fat; 207 calories
tips: Salad is best made close to serving time. Dressing can be made a day ahead; cover, refrigerate.

Rigatoni with Tomato and Avocado

preparation time 15 minutes

cooking time 15 minutes

1 lb. rigatoni pasta
$1/4$ cup olive oil
14-oz. can whole tomatoes, drained
$1 1/2$ tbsp. tomato paste
$1 1/2$ tbsp. lemon juice
5 medium plum tomatoes, seeded, chopped finely
1 small red onion, chopped finely
$1/4$ cup coarsely chopped fresh parsley
2 serrano chiles, seeded, chopped finely
1 clove garlic, crushed
$1/4$ cup pine nuts, toasted
1 cup kalamata olives
1 medium avocado, chopped coarsely

Cook pasta in large pot of boiling salted water, uncovered, until just tender; drain. Transfer pasta to large bowl; stir in oil.

Meanwhile, blend or process tomatoes, paste and lemon juice until smooth.

Combine tomato mixture and all remaining ingredients except avocado in large bowl. Add pasta and gently toss to combine. Stir avocado through just before serving.

SERVES 4

per serving: 32.6g fat; 774 calories
tip: This recipe is best made close to serving time.

Tofu and Vegetable Stir-fry

12 oz. cauliflower, chopped
12 oz. broccoli, chopped
8 oz. asparagus, sliced
12 oz. green beans, sliced
4 large carrots, sliced
$1/4$ cup olive oil
2 cloves garlic, crushed
$1^{1}/2$ tbsp. chopped fresh thyme
1 tsp. cracked black pepper
13-oz. package firm tofu, cubed
2 medium onions, sliced
8 oz. button mushrooms, sliced
$1/4$ cup white wine
$1/2$ cup vegetable stock
$1/4$ cup (1 oz.) freshly grated parmesan cheese

Cook cauliflower, broccoli, asparagus, beans and carrots in large pot of boiling water, about two minutes; drain, rinse, drain.

Heat oil in large skillet; cook garlic, thyme, pepper and tofu until tofu is lightly browned. Remove, keep warm.

Add onions and mushrooms to same skillet; cook until onions are soft. Add vegetable mixture, wine and stock; stir until sauce boils and thickens slightly. Stir in tofu.

Serve sprinkled with cheese.

SERVES 6

per serving: 15.2g fat; 259 calories
tip: This recipe is best made close to serving time.

Beans with Tomatoes, Feta and Olives

preparation time 10 minutes
cooking time 15 minutes

2 tsp. olive oil
$1/4$ cup pine nuts
14 oz. green beans, halved
1 clove garlic, crushed
6 medium plum tomatoes (about 1 lb.),
  roughly chopped
$1/2$ cup seeded black olives
$10^{1}/2$-oz. can red kidney beans, rinsed, drained
3 tbsp. dry white wine
$1^{1}/2$ tbsp. lemon juice
2 tsp. chopped fresh thyme
2 tsp. honey
7 oz. feta cheese, crumbled

Heat oil in large skillet; cook pine nuts until lightly browned. Remove from skillet.

Add green beans and garlic to same skillet; stir-fry. Add tomatoes; stir-fry.

Add olives to skillet with kidney beans, wine, lemon juice, thyme and honey; stir until hot. Stir in pine nuts and cheese.

SERVES 6

per serving: 14.5g fat; 236 calories
tip: This recipe is best made close to serving time.

Gado Gado Stir-fry

preparation time 15 minutes

cooking time 15 minutes

8 oz. cauliflower, chopped
8 oz. broccoli, chopped
$1^{1}/_{2}$ tbsp. peanut oil
1 medium onion, sliced
1 medium red bell pepper, sliced
5 oz. green beans, sliced
$1^{1}/_{4}$ lbs. Chinese cabbage, shredded
$10^{1}/_{2}$-oz. can garbanzos, rinsed, drained
2 cups bean sprouts
2 cups coconut milk
$^{3}/_{4}$ cup chunky-style peanut butter
1 clove garlic, crushed
2 tbsp. soy sauce
2 tsp. lemon juice
$^{1}/_{4}$ tsp. mild chili powder

Gado gado is an Indonesian dish of cooked vegetables served with a peanut sauce.

Boil, steam or microwave cauliflower and broccoli separately until just tender; drain.

Heat oil in large skillet; cook onion, bell pepper and beans until onion is soft.

Add cabbage and garbanzos to skillet; cook until cabbage is just wilted. Add cauliflower, broccoli and sprouts; cook until hot. Remove; keep warm. Add remaining ingredients to same skillet; cook, stirring, until sauce boils. Serve sauce over vegetables.

SERVES 4

per serving: 53.3g fat; 693 calories
tip: This recipe is best made close to serving time.

Gnocchi with Spinach, Tomato and Pine Nuts

preparation time 10 minutes

cooking time 15 minutes

$3/4$ cup heavy cream
15-oz. can crushed tomatoes, undrained
3 cloves garlic, crushed
$1/2$ cup drained chopped sun-dried tomatoes in oil
$1/2$ cup seeded black olives, sliced
$1^3/4$ lbs. packaged potato gnocchi
1 lb. spinach, chopped coarsely
$1/2$ cup pine nuts, toasted

Gnocchi are the Italian version of dumplings; the most common types are made of potato, semolina or ricotta and spinach. They are available, ready-made, from the refrigerated sections of some supermarkets. If you can't find them fresh in your area, dried gnocchi will work well. We used a potato gnocchi here.

Place cream, tomatoes and garlic in large pot, bring to a boil; simmer, uncovered, about five minutes or until sauce thickens slightly. Add sun-dried tomatoes and olives; simmer, uncovered, two minutes.

Meanwhile, cook gnocchi according to package directions; drain.

Gently toss gnocchi, spinach and pine nuts with sauce in pot until spinach wilts and mixture is heated through.

SERVES 4

per serving: 37.5g fat; 690 calories
tip: This recipe is best made close to serving time.

Olive, Onion and Tomato Salad

preparation time 15 minutes

no coooking time required

8 medium tomatoes (about $3^1/_2$ lbs.)
1 large red onion, sliced
2 cups seeded black olives
1 cup firmly packed fresh basil, shredded

DRESSING
$^1/_4$ cup olive oil
$1^1/_2$ tbsp. balsamic vinegar
$^1/_2$ tsp. sugar
$1^1/_2$ tbsp. Dijon mustard

Quarter tomatoes lengthwise, remove seeds; slice each quarter in half lengthwise.

Whisk together ingredients for dressing.

Combine tomatoes with remaining ingredients in large bowl; add dressing, mix gently.

SERVES 6

per serving: 10.1g fat; 189 calories
tip: This recipe can be prepared up to
two hours ahead; cover, refrigerate.
Add dressing just before serving.

Roman-style Green Beans

preparation time 15 minutes

cooking time 10 minutes

3 slices prosciutto
1 lb. green beans
3 tbsp. olive oil
7 oz. button mushrooms
3 tbsp. pine nuts, toasted
1$\frac{1}{2}$ tbsp. lemon juice
6 sprigs fresh thyme
pinch grated lemon peel

Cook prosciutto under hot broiler until crisp; drain on paper towels. Snap prosciutto into small pieces; reserve.

Trim stem ends of beans.

Heat oil in large skillet, add mushrooms; cook one minute. Add beans; cook about three minutes or until just tender. Add prosciutto, pine nuts, lemon juice, thyme and lemon peel; toss mixture gently until heated through.

SERVES 6

per serving: 10.2g fat; 123 calories
tip: This recipe is best made just before serving time.

Rice & Noodles

Beef and Green beans with Noodles

preparation time 10 minutes
(plus standing time)

cooking time 20 minutes

8 oz. rice vermicelli noodles
2 tbsp. peanut oil
2 medium onions, sliced
3 tbsp. red wine vinegar
$1^{1}/_{2}$ tbsp. brown sugar
$1^{1}/_{4}$ lbs. beef tenderloin, sliced thinly
2 tsp. grated fresh ginger
3 cloves garlic, crushed
$^{1}/_{4}$ cup hoisin sauce
3 tbsp. light soy sauce
3 tbsp. chopped fresh cilantro
12 oz. green beans, chopped
$1^{1}/_{2}$ tbsp. sesame seeds

Place noodles in heatproof bowl, cover with boiling water, let stand five minutes; drain.

Heat one teaspoon oil in large skillet, add onions, vinegar and sugar; cook over low heat, stirring occasionally, until onions are caramelized; remove.

Heat all but one teaspoon oil in wok; add beef in batches, stir-fry until browned and tender; remove from wok.

Heat remaining teaspoon of oil in wok, add ginger, garlic, sauces, cilantro, beans and sesame seeds, stir-fry until beans are just tender. Return beef and onions to wok with noodles, stir until heated through.

SERVES 4

per serving: 17.6g fat; 552 calories
tip: This recipe is best made close to serving time.

Pork, Pine Nut and Cointreau Risotto

preparation time 10 minutes

cooking time 30 minutes

1 lb. boneless pork chops
1 1/2 tbsp. teriyaki sauce
1 tsp. finely grated orange peel
3 cloves garlic, crushed
1 large onion, chopped finely
2 cups arborio rice
5 cups chicken stock
1/2 cup dry white wine
3 tbsp. cointreau
5 cups baby spinach leaves
3 tbsp. pine nuts, toasted
3 tbsp. coarsely chopped fresh thyme
1 pinch grated lemon peel

Preheat oven to 450°F.

Place pork on rack in baking dish; brush with combined teriyaki sauce and orange peel. Bake, uncovered, 20 minutes. Cover pork, let stand five minutes; slice thinly.

Meanwhile, cook garlic and onion in large, heated oiled pot, stirring, until onion softens. Add rice, stock, wine and cointreau, bring to a boil; simmer, covered, 15 minutes, stirring midway through cooking. Remove from heat; let stand, covered, 10 minutes. Gently stir in spinach, pine nuts, thyme, lemon peel and pork.

SERVES 4

per serving: 10g fat; 663 calories
tip: This recipe is best made close to serving time.

Seafood Paella

preparation time 20 minutes

cooking time 25 minutes

1 lb. large mussels
1/4 cup olive oil
1 medium onion, chopped finely
2 cloves garlic, chopped
1 boneless, skinless chicken breast, sliced
1 medium red bell pepper, chopped
1 medium green bell pepper, chopped
3 medium tomatoes (about 1 1/4 lbs.),
  seeded, chopped
1 tsp. sugar
2 cups long-grain rice
3 1/2 cups chicken stock
1/4 tsp. ground saffron
2 bay leaves
10 1/2 oz. ocean trout fillet, chopped
5 oz. white fish fillet, chopped
10 1/2 oz. cooked shrimp, shelled, chopped

Scrub mussels, remove beards.

Heat oil in large pot, add onion and garlic; cook, stirring, until onion is soft. Add chicken and bell peppers; cook, stirring, one minute. Stir in tomatoes and sugar, bring to a boil; simmer, uncovered, until almost all liquid has evaporated.

Stir in rice, stock, saffron and bay leaves, stir until boiling; simmer, covered, 10 minutes. Stir in mussels, top with fish and shrimp, cover, simmer about five minutes or until fish is cooked. Gently stir fish and shrimp through rice before serving.

SERVES 6

per serving: 14.8g fat; 526 calories
tip: This recipe is best made close to serving time.

Chili Chicken Noodle Stir-fry

preparation time 10 minutes
(plus standing time)

cooking time 15 minutes

3 tbsp. finely chopped fresh cilantro
2 cloves garlic, crushed
4 serrano chiles, chopped finely
4 boneless, skinless chicken thighs (15 oz.), sliced thinly
two 3-oz. packages instant Raman noodles
3 tbsp. vegetable oil
1 medium onion, sliced thinly
1 large red bell pepper, sliced thinly
12 oz. baby tat soi, chopped coarsely
2 cups mixed salad greens
2 scallions, sliced thinly
3 tbsp. oyster sauce

Tat soi is an Asian green vegetable. It can be replaced with Chinese broccoli or spinach leaves, if you prefer

Combine cilantro, garlic and chilies in large bowl; add chicken, toss to coat in marinade. Cover; refrigerate 10 minutes.

Discard seasoning packets from noodles; cook noodles according to instructions on package, drain.

Heat half the oil in large skillet; cook chicken, in batches, until browned and cooked through. Heat remaining oil in same skillet; cook onion and bell pepper two minutes. Return chicken to skillet with noodles; cook two minutes. Add tat soi, salad greens, scallions and oyster sauce; cook until leaves are just wilted.

SERVES 4

per serving: 25.7g fat; 466 calories
tips: Chicken can be marinated several hours or overnight; cover, refrigerate. Chicken can also be frozen for up to two months.

Sang Choy Bow

preparation time 20 minutes

cooking time 15 minutes

4 dried shiitake mushrooms
$1^1/_2$ tbsp. peanut oil
7 oz. ground pork
7 oz. ground chicken
6 scallions, chopped coarsely
1 clove garlic, crushed
$^1/_4$ cup canned drained bamboo shoots, chopped finely
8-oz. can water chestnuts, drained, chopped coarsely
2 tsp. sesame oil
3 tbsp. light soy sauce
3 tbsp. oyster sauce
2 tsp. cornstarch
$1^1/_2$ tbsp. dry sherry
$3^1/_2$ oz. fried noodles
1 cup bean sprouts, chopped coarsely
2 scallions, sliced thinly, extra
8 large iceberg lettuce leaves

Sang choy bow is that delicious Chinese dish in which well-seasoned diced or ground meat is wrapped in cool lettuce leaves. The noodles used here are sold in Asian markets as 'fried crispy egg noodles.'

Place mushrooms in small heatproof bowl; cover with boiling water. Let stand 20 minutes; drain. Discard stems; chop caps coarsely.

Heat peanut oil in large skillet; cook pork and chicken until cooked through. Add mushrooms, scallions, garlic, shoots, chestnuts, sesame oil, sauces and blended cornstarch and sherry; cook, stirring, two minutes. Just before serving, stir in noodles, sprouts and extra scallions.

Divide mixture among lettuce leaves to serve.

SERVES 4

per serving: 18.1g fat 322 calories
tip: This recipe is best made close to serving time.

Satay Beef and Noodle Stir-fry

preparation time 5 minutes

cooking time 10 minutes

1 lb. Asian stir-fry noodles
$1^{1}/_{2}$ tbsp. peanut oil
$1^{3}/_{4}$ lbs. beef strips
2 cloves garlic, crushed
$1^{1}/_{2}$ cups bottled satay sauce
1-lb. package frozen stir-fry vegetables, thawed
$^{1}/_{4}$ cup finely chopped fresh cilantro

Asian stir-fry noodles (also called hokkien noodles) and bottled satay sauce can be found in the international isles of most supermarkets.

Pour boiling water over noodles in large heatproof bowl; separate noodles with a fork, drain.

Heat half the oil in large skillet; cook beef, in batches, until browned all over and just cooked.

Add remaining oil to skillet, add garlic; cook, stirring, until fragrant. Add satay sauce; cook one minute. Return beef to pan with noodles and vegetables; cook, stirring, until heated through. Stir in cilantro. Garnish with cilantro sprigs and bean sprouts, if desired.

SERVES 4

per serving: 42g fat; 796 calories
tips: This recipe is best made close to serving time.

Combination Chow Mein

preparation time 10 minutes

cooking time 30 minutes

vegetable oil for deep-frying
7 oz. dried chow mein noodles
1/4 cup light soy sauce
1 1/2 tbsp. oyster sauce
3 tbsp. peanut oil
2 cloves garlic, crushed
1 1/2 tbsp. grated fresh ginger
1 large red bell pepper, sliced
8-oz. can water chestnuts,
  drained, sliced

6 scallions, sliced finely
3 oz. bean sprouts
3 boneless, skinless chicken breasts
  (1 lb.), sliced into 2" pieces
1/3 cup chopped fresh chives
1 1/4 lbs. medium uncooked shrimp
8 oz. Chinese cabbage, shredded
1/2 tsp. sesame oil
2 tsp. cornstarch
1/2 cup chicken stock

Heat vegetable oil in large pot; deep-fry noodles, in batches, until puffed. Drain noodles on paper towels. Peel and devein shrimp, leaving tails intact.

Heat half the peanut oil in large skillet; cook chicken, in batches, until browned on both sides and tender. Cover chicken to keep warm. Add shrimp to same skillet; cook, stirring, until shrimp change color. Remove from skillet; cover.

Heat remaining peanut oil in same skillet; cook garlic, ginger, bell pepper, water chestnuts and all but 1 1/2 tablespoons of the scallions until bell pepper is just tender.

Return chicken and shrimp to skillet; add cabbage, sprouts and chives, cook until cabbage is just wilted.

Stir in combined sauces, sesame oil and blended cornstarch and stock; cook, stirring, until mixture boils and thickens. Serve with deep-fried noodles; sprinkle with remaining scallions.

SERVES 6

per serving: 14.9g fat; 321 calories
tip: This recipe is best made close to serving time.

Sausage Risotto

preparation time 10 minutes

cooking time 35 minutes

1 lb. beef sausages
4 small tomatoes (about 1 lb.)
3 tbsp. olive oil
1 large leek, chopped coarsely
1 clove garlic, crushed
$1/4$ cup dry red wine
2 cups arborio rice
8 cups boiling beef stock
$1/2$ cup (2 oz.) freshly grated
  parmesan cheese
$1^{1}/2$ tbsp. finely chopped fresh parsley

Preheat oven to 400°F.

Cook sausages in heated oiled skillet until browned all over and cooked through; slice thickly.

Meanwhile, cut tomatoes into wedges; place wedges on baking sheet, brush with half the oil. Bake about 15 minutes or until softened.

Heat remaining oil in large pot; cook leek and garlic, stirring, until leek is soft. Add wine; simmer until liquid is reduced by half. Stir in rice and stock; simmer, uncovered, stirring occasionally, about 25 minutes or until most of liquid is absorbed and rice is just tender. Just before serving, stir in sausages, tomatoes, cheese and parsley.

SERVES 4

per serving: 46g fat; 921 calories
tips: This recipe is best made close to serving time. Sausages and tomatoes can be cooked a day ahead; cover, refrigerate.

Honeyed Scallop and Chili Stir-fry

preparation time 10 minutes

cooking time 10 minutes

1 1/4 lbs. fresh or dried egg noodles
3 tsp. peanut oil
1 medium onion, quartered
2 medium red bell peppers, sliced thinly
1 trimmed celery stalk, sliced
3 1/2 oz. snow peas
7 oz. scallops
1 1/2 tbsp. honey
1 tsp. Asian-style chili sauce
2 tsp. chopped fresh mint

Cook noodles in a large pot of boiling water, uncovered, until just tender; drain.

Meanwhile, heat oil in large skillet, add vegetables; cook, stirring, over high heat one minute. Add remaining ingredients; cook, stirring, two minutes or until scallops are tender. Add noodles; toss well.

SERVES 4

per serving: 5g fat; 319 calories
tip: This recipe is best made close to serving time.

Eggs

Spanish Potato Omelet

preparation time 10 minutes
(plus standing time)

cooking time 35 minutes

5 large potatoes (about $3\frac{1}{2}$ lbs.)
1 medium onion, sliced thinly
olive oil for frying
8 eggs, beaten lightly
1 tsp. sweet paprika
$\frac{1}{4}$ cup olive oil, extra

Peel potatoes and cut into very thin slices; pat dry with paper towels. Fry potatoes and onion in hot oil, in batches, until just soft but not browned. Transfer potatoes and onion to strainer; cool. Place potatoes and onion in large bowl, add combined eggs and paprika; let stand five minutes.

Heat extra oil in 10-inch non-stick skillet. Pour in potato mixture, press down firmly. Cook, uncovered, over low heat, about 15 minutes or until potatoes are soft and base of omelet is browned.

Carefully invert potato omelet onto large plate; slide back into same skillet. Cook, uncovered, over low heat, about 10 minutes or until base is browned and omelet set. Let stand for 10 minutes; cut into wedges.

SERVES 8

per serving: 23.6g fat; 36 calories
tip: This recipe is best made close to serving time.

Giant Denver Omelets

preparation time 10 minutes
cooking time 25 minutes

10 eggs, beaten lightly
1 1/2 tbsp. whole-grain mustard

DENVER FILLING
2 tsp. vegetable oil
1 large onion, sliced thinly
1 medium red bell pepper, sliced thinly
3 1/2 oz. ham, sliced thinly
1/4 cup finely chopped fresh parsley
2 small tomatoes, seeded, sliced thinly
1/2 cup (2 oz.) shredded cheddar cheese

Make Denver filling, then combine eggs and mustard in large measuring cup or small bowl.

Heat nine-inch non-stick skillet; coat with cooking-oil spray. Pour $1/4$ cup of the egg mixture into skillet; cook, tilting skillet, over medium heat until almost set. Sprinkle $1/3$ cup Denver filling over half the omelet; using a spatula, fold omelet in half to enclose filling.

Pour another $1/4$ cup of egg mixture into empty half of skillet; mixture will spread under the first folded omelet. Cook over high heat until almost set.

Sprinkle omelet with another $1/3$ cup of Denver filling, fold omelet over, onto the top of the first folded omelet. Repeat this process two more times to complete one giant layered omelet. Carefully slide omelet onto plate; keep warm. Repeat layering process to make second omelet with remaining egg mixture and filling. Cut omelets in half to serve.

Denver Filling: Heat oil in medium skillet; cook onion and bell pepper, stirring, until onion is soft. Combine onion mixture with remaining ingredients in medium bowl.

SERVES 4

per serving: 22.3g fat; 336 calories
tips: This recipe is best made close to serving time. Filling can be made several hours ahead; cover, refrigerate.

Souffle Omelet with Mushroom Sauce

preparation time 15 minutes

cooking time 35 minutes

4 eggs, separated
1 1/2 tbsp. water
2 tsp. chopped fresh tarragon
1 1/2 tbsp. butter

MUSHROOM SAUCE
5 tbsp. butter
1 small onion, chopped
1 clove garlic, crushed
4 oz. button mushrooms, sliced
3 tsp. flour
1/4 cup dry white wine
1/2 cup chicken stock
1/4 cup milk
2 tsp. yellow mustard
2 tsp. chopped fresh tarragon

Make mushroom sauce. Meanwhile, whisk egg yolks, water and tarragon in large bowl until well combined. Beat egg whites in small bowl with electric mixer until soft peaks form. Fold egg whites gently into egg yolk mixture in two batches.

Heat half the butter in ovenproof omelet pan, pour in half the egg mixture; cook omelet until lightly browned underneath. Place pan under hot broiler until top of omelet is just set. Slide omelet onto serving plate, fold omelet in half, spoon half the mushroom sauce over it. Repeat with remaining butter, egg mixture and sauce.

Mushroom Sauce: Heat butter in skillet, add onion, garlic and mushrooms; cook, stirring, until onion is soft. Add flour, cook, stirring, until combined. Remove from heat, gradually stir in combined remaining ingredients; stir over medium heat until mixture boils and thickens.

SERVES 2

per serving: 45.1g fat; 533 calories
tips: Omelets are best made close to serving time. Mushroom sauce can be made a day ahead; cover, refrigerate.

Potato Cakes with Spinach and Poached Eggs

preparation time 20 minutes
cooking time 20 minutes

4 medium potatoes (about 1³/4 lbs.), grated
1 small onion, grated
1 egg, beaten lightly
¹/3 cup flour
3 tbsp. vegetable oil
1 lb. spinach, shredded
4 eggs, extra
10¹/2 oz. sliced smoked salmon

TOMATO HOLLANDAISE SAUCE
2 egg yolks
1¹/2 tbsp. white wine vinegar
2 sticks butter, melted
2 tsp. chopped fresh tarragon
1 small tomato, peeled, seeded, chopped

Combine potatoes, onion, egg and flour in large bowl. Heat oil in large skillet; cook ³/4-cups of mixture until crisp and golden on both sides. Set aside; keep warm.

Meanwhile, boil, steam or microwave spinach until just wilted. Poach eggs in large pot of simmering water until cooked as desired.

Make tomato hollandaise sauce. Serve potato cakes topped with spinach, smoked salmon and eggs; pour tomato hollandaise sauce over all.

Tomato Hollandaise Sauce: Blend egg yolks and vinegar until combined. Continue to blend while gradually adding butter in a thin stream (do not add white milky residue). Stir in tarragon and tomato.

SERVES **4**

per serving: 74.1g fat; 966 calories
tip: This recipe is best made close to serving time.

Basic Mayonnaise
preparation time 5 min.

2 egg yolks • 1^1/2 tbsp. lemon juice • 1 tsp. Dijon mustard • ^{1}/2 cup olive oil • ^{1}/2 cup light olive oil • 3 tbsp. h
water, approximately

Blend or process egg yolks, lemon juice and mustard until smooth. Add combined oils gradually in a thin stream wh
motor is running; add enough water to bring mayonnaise to desired consistency. Blend until smooth. **Makes abo
1 cup. per 1^1/2 tbsp.: 19.9g fat; 180 calories. Tip: This recipe can be made a week ahead; cover, refrigerat**

Pesto
preparation time 20 min.

4 cups firmly packed fresh basil • 1 cup pine nuts, toasted • 4 cloves garlic, chopped • 1 cup olive oil • ^{2}/3 c
(about 2^1/2 oz.) freshly grated parmesan cheese • olive oil, extra

Process basil, nuts and garlic until finely chopped. Add oil in thin stream while motor is running, process ur
combined. Add cheese, process until mixture is combined. Spoon pesto into hot sterilized jars; drizzle a thin la
of extra oil over top to cover pesto, leaving 1^1/4-inch space between oil and top of jars. Seal jars. **Makes abo
2^1/2 cups. per 1^1/2 tbsp.: 20.8g fat; 196 calories. Tips: This recipe is best made a day ahead; refrigerate. Pes
can also be frozen for up to six months.**

Italian Dressing
preparation time 5 min.

^{1}/3 cup olive oil • ^{1}/3 cup vegetable oil • ^{1}/4 cup white vinegar • 1 tsp. sugar • 1^1/2 tbsp. Dijon mustard • 1 clove
garlic, crushed

Combine all ingredients in a large measuring cup. Whisk well before use. **Makes about 1 cup. per 1^1/2 tbsp.: 12.:
fat; 111 calories. Tip: This recipe can be made a week ahead; cover, refrigerate.**

Low-fat Salad Dressing
preparation time 5 min.

^{1}/3 cup buttermilk • ^{1}/3 cup low-fat yogurt • 1^1/2 tbsp. water • 3 tbsp. lemon juice

Combine all ingredients in measuring cup or small bowl; mix well. **Makes about 1 cup. per 1^1/2 tbsp.: 02.g f:
9 calories. Tip: This recipe can be made two days ahead; cover, refrigerate. Mix well before use.**

Fresh Tomato Pasta Sauce
preparation time 15 min. • cooking time 30 min.

tbsp. olive oil • 1 large onion, chopped • 2 cloves garlic, crushed • 10 medium tomatoes (about 4^1/2 lbs.), peeled, opped • 2 tsp. salt • ^{1}/2 cup dry red wine • 2 tsp. brown sugar • 3 tbsp. tomato paste • 3 tbsp. finely chopped fresh sil leaves • 3 tbsp. finely chopped fresh parsley • 2 tsp. finely chopped fresh oregano • ^{1}/2 tsp. cracked black peppercorns

at oil in large pot; cook onion and garlic, stirring, until onion is soft. Add tomatoes, salt and wine; simmer, covered, about 15 minutes or until tomatoes are soft. Add remaining ingredients to pan; simmer, uncovered, out 10 minutes or until thickened. Pour sauce into hot sterilized bottles; seal immediately. kes about 7 cups. **per cup: 5.6g fat; 114 calories. Tip: This recipe is best made a day ahead; refrigerate.**

Caesar Dressing
preparation time 5 min. • cooking time 10 min.

gg • 8 anchovy fillets, chopped • 2 cloves garlic, crushed • 3 tbsp. lemon juice • ^{1}/2 cup (2 oz.) freshly grated parmesan eese • ^{1}/2 tsp. cracked black pepper • ^{3}/4 cup olive oil • ^{1}/3 cup heavy cream

en a recipe calls for a soft-boiled egg, use the method illustrated in this recipe. Bring a small pot of water a boil. Add egg, immediately remove pot from heat; cover, let stand three minutes. Drain; cool egg under ning water, peel over small bowl. Whisk together egg, anchovies, garlic, lemon juice, cheese and pepper. dually add oil in a thin stream, whisking well. Whisk in cream. **Makes about 1^1/2 cups. per 1^1/2 tbsp.: 12.2g ; 117 calories. Tip: This recipe can be made three hours ahead; cover, refrigerate.**

Blender Hollandaise
preparation time 5 min.

gg yolks • 3 tbsp. lemon juice • 1 stick butter, melted

e amount of butter used in the blender is only about half the amount the egg yolks could absorb if the sauce re made by hand. If more than one stick of butter is used, the sauce will be too thick. Stir in one to three lespoons of hot water if sauce is too thick to pour. Blend or process yolks and juice for five seconds. With motor ning, pour hot bubbling butter into egg mixture in a slow steady stream (it should take about 15 seconds). Omit butter's milky residue at the bottom of the pot. **Makes about 1 cup. per 1^1/2 tbsp.: 10g fat; 93 calories. : This recipe can be made one hour ahead; store at room temperature.**

Glossary

Almonds ground: also known as almond meal, almonds powdered to a flour-like texture; used in baking or as a thickening agent.

Bean sprouts: new growths of assorted beans and seeds germinated for consumption as sprouts. The most readily available are alfalfa, mung bean and soy bean sprouts.

Breadcrumbs: *Packaged:* fine-textured, crunchy, purchased white breadcrumbs. *Stale:* one- or two-day-old bread made into crumbs by grating, blending or processing.

Buttermilk: sold alongside fresh milk products in supermarkets; despite the implication of its name, it is low in fat. Commercially made by a method similar to yogurt, buttermilk is a good low-fat substitute for dairy products such as cream or sour cream; good in baking and in salad dressings.

Cabbage, Chinese: also known as Peking cabbage.

Cajun seasoning: used to give an authentic 'Deep South' spicy flavor to food; packaged blend of herbs and spices that can include paprika, basil, onion, fennel, thyme, cayenne pepper and tarragon.

Capers: the gray-green buds of a warm climate (usually Mediterranean) shrub, used to enhance dressings and sauces with their piquancy. Sold either dried and salted or pickled in a vinegar brine. If salted, rinse and drain before use; if pickled, drain before use.

Chilies: available in many varieties and sizes. Use rubber gloves when seeding and chopping fresh chilies as they can burn your skin. Removing seeds and membranes before use lessens the heat level of your dish. *Flakes:* crushed, dried chlies. *Serrano:* small, thin-fleshed red chili with a fiery heat. *Thai:* small chilies that are medium to hot in flavor, and bright red to dark green in color.

Coconut: *Cream:* the first pressing from grated mature coconut flesh. *Milk:* the second pressing (less rich) from grated mature coconut flesh. A low-fat variety of coconut milk is also available.

Corn Flakes, crushed: crushed Corn Flakes cereal; can be used in place of breadcrumbs.

Cornstarch: used as a thickening agent in cooking.

Couscous: a fine, grain-like cereal product, originally from North Africa; made from semolina.

Curry paste: red commercially packaged product containing red chilies and a variety of other herbs and spices.

Mango chutney: commercially packaged product based on mango and various spices; traditionally served with Indian food, but is also good with cold meats, salads or cheeses.

Milk, evaporated: canned product available (regular and fat-free) in supermarkets.

Mirin: a sweet, low-alcohol rice wine used in Japanese cooking; sometimes referred to simply as rice wine; should not be confused with sake, the Japanese rice wine made for drinking.

Mushrooms: *Cremini:* light to dark brown in color with a mild, earthy flavor. *Oyster:* also called abalone mushroom, they are gray-white in color and shaped like a fan. *Shiitake:* cultivated mushroom with a rich, meaty flavor; available fresh and dried. Dried shiitake mushrooms should reconstituted before using by soaking in boiling water.

Mustard: *Dijon:* a pale brown, distinctively-flavored, fairly mild French mustard. *Whole-grain:* French-style coarse grained mustard made from crushed mustard seeds and n-style French mustard. The seeds can be black or ⌐w. **Yellow:** smooth, sweet mustard made with mustard ⌐ds, malt vinegar, caramel, herbs and spices.

Cooking-oil spray: available from supermarkets in ⌐sol cans. **Sesame:** made from roasted, crushed white ⌐me seeds; a flavoring rather than a cooking medium.

⌐on: **Green:** also known as scallion or, incorrectly, shallot; ⌐nmature onion picked before the bulb has formed, having ⌐ng, bright-green edible stalk. **Red:** also known as ⌐nish, red Spanish or Bermuda onion; a sweet-flavored, ⌐e, purple-red onion that is particularly good eaten raw in ⌐ds. **White:** interchangeable with yellow onions; the ⌐gent flesh adds flavor to a vast range of dishes.

⌐rika: packaged powder made by grinding aromatic ⌐et red pepper pods. The two blends available are hot, ⌐h is fiery, and sweet, which is mild.

⌐cetta: an Italian salt-cured pork roll, usually cut from ⌐belly; used, chopped, in cooked dishes to add flavor. ⌐on can be substituted.

⌐per, **lemon:** a packaged blend of crushed black ⌐percorns, lemon, herbs and spices.

⌐nta: a flour-like cereal made from ground corn; similar to ⌐meal, but finer. Also the name of the dish made from it.

⌐, **garlic:** packaged blend of salt and ground, dehydrated ⌐c, available in supermarkets.

⌐ce: **Fish:** made from salted, pulverized, fermented ⌐l fish, often anchovies. Has pungent smell and strong ⌐e; use sparingly. **Oyster:** Asian in origin, this rich brown ⌐e is made from oysters and their brine, cooked with ⌐and soy sauce, then thickened with starch. **Satay:** commercially prepared spicy sauce, originating in South-East Asia, based on peanuts and a variety of herbs and spices. **Sweet Thai chili:** relatively mild, Thai-type sauce made from red chilies, sugar, garlic and vinegar. **Tabasco:** brand name of an extremely fiery sauce made from vinegar, hot red peppers and salt. **Teriyaki:** a sauce consisting of soy sauce, corn syrup, vinegar, ginger and spices; also the name of a distinctive glaze on grilled meats.

Soup, condensed tomato: commercially made concentrated soup, available in supermarkets.

Star anise: a dried, star-shaped pod whose seeds have an astringent aniseed flavor.

Sugar, brown: an extremely soft, finely granulated sugar retaining molasses for its characteristic color and flavor.

Sun-dried tomatoes: halved, dehydrated tomatoes available loose and bottled in oil.

Sun-dried tomato paste: commercially produced paste made from sun-dried tomatoes, oil, garlic, basil, salt, pine nuts and spices; available in delicatessens and some supermarkets.

Taco seasoning: a packaged seasoning made from oregano, cumin, chilies and other spices.

Tomato: *Pasta sauce:* prepared, bottled sauce of crushed tomatoes and various spices and herbs. **Paste:** triple-concentrated tomato puree used to flavor soups, stews and sauces. **Puree:** canned, pureed tomatoes (not tomato paste). Substitute with fresh peeled and pureed tomatoes.

Vinegar, white wine: vinegar made from white wine.

Water chestnuts: crunchy, nutty-tasting tuber with brownish-black skin and white flesh; available fresh or canned.

Time Inc. Home Entertainment
Publisher Richard Fraiman
Executive Director, Marketing Services Carol Pittard
Director, Retail & Special Sales Tom Mifsud
Marketing Director, Branded Businesses Swati Rao
Director, New Product Development Peter Harper
Assistant Financial Director Steven Sandonato
Prepress Manager Emily Rabin
Product Manager Victoria Alfonso
Associate Book Production Manager Suzanne Janso
Associate Prepress Manager Anne-Michelle Gallero

special thanks: Bozena Bannett, Alexandra Bliss, Glenn Buonocore, Bernadette Corbie, Robert Marasco, Brooke McGuire, Jonathan Polsky, Ilene Schreider, Adriana Tierno

Cover and interior design by Emily Rabin

Published by Time Inc. Home Entertainment
© ACP Magazines Ltd 2005

Time Inc., 1271 Avenue of the Americas, New York, New York 10020

ISBN: 1-932994-30-0

We welcome your comments and suggestions about Time Inc. Home Entertainment. Please write to us at: Time Inc. Home Entertainment, Attention: Book Editors, P.O. Box 11016, Des Moines, IA 50336-1016.

If you would like to order any of our hardcover Collector's Edition books, please call us at 1-800-327-6388. (Monday through Friday, 7:00 a.m.— 8:00 p.m. or Saturday, 7:00 a.m.— 6:00 p.m. Central Time).

Fast & Fabulous: Delicious Meals Without the Wait
First published by ACP Magazines Ltd 2000

Food Director Pamela Clark
Photographers Steve Brown, Scott Cameron, Robert Clark, Robert Taylor, Ian Wallace
Stylists Clare Bradford, Carolyn Fienberg, Kay Francis, Jane Hann, Cherise Koch, Vicki Liley, Michelle Noerianto, Sarah O'Brien

Managing Editor Susan Tomnay
Publisher Sue Wannan